MW01061931

Seven Events
THAT SHAPED THE
New Testament
World

Seven Events

THAT SHAPED THE

New Testament World

WARREN CARTER

Baker Academic

a division of Baker Publishing Group
Grand Rapids, Michigan

© 2013 by Warren Carter

Published by Baker Academic
a division of Baker Publishing Group
P.O. Box 6287, Grand Rapids, MI 49516-6287
www.bakeracademic.com

Printed in the United States of America

All rights reserved. No part of this publication may be reproduced, stored in a retrieval system, or transmitted in any form or by any means—for example, electronic, photocopy, recording—without the prior written permission of the publisher. The only exception is brief quotations in printed reviews.

Library of Congress Cataloging-in-Publication Data

Carter, Warren, 1955–
        Seven events that shaped the New Testament world / Warren Carter.
        p. cm.
        Includes index.
        ISBN 978-0-8010-3916-4 (pbk.)
        1. Bible—History of contemporary events. 2. Bible. N.T.—History of contemporary events. 3. Church history—Primitive and early church, ca. 30–600. I. Title.
BS635.3.C37 2013
225.9′5—dc23   2012035263

Unless otherwise indicated, Scripture quotations are from the New Revised Standard Version of the Bible, copyright © 1989, by the Division of Christian Education of the National Council of the Churches of Christ in the United States of America. Used by permission. All rights reserved.

Scripture quotations labeled NIV are from the Holy Bible, New International Version®. NIV®. Copyright © 1973, 1978, 1984, 2011 by Biblica, Inc.™ Used by permission of Zondervan. All rights reserved worldwide. www.zondervan.com

Scripture quotations labeled RSV are from the Revised Standard Version of the Bible, copyright 1952 [2nd edition, 1971] by the Division of Christian Education of the National Council of the Churches of Christ in the United States of America. Used by permission. All rights reserved.

The internet addresses, email addresses, and phone numbers in this book are accurate at the time of publication. They are provided as a resource. Baker Publishing Group does not endorse them or vouch for their content or permanence.

In keeping with biblical principles of creation stewardship, Baker Publishing Group advocates the responsible use of our natural resources. As a member of the Green Press Initiative, our company uses recycled paper when possible. The text paper of this book is composed in part of post-consumer waste.

14   15   16   17   18   19   7   6   5   4   3   2

For Lee—
with whom I have experienced
many wonderful events

CONTENTS

ILLUSTRATIONS

PREFACE

*F*irst, a word of explanation. In this book I refer to dates using the abbreviation of BCE and CE. These abbreviations may not be familiar to some readers. BCE stands for "before the Common Era." CE is an abbreviation for "Common Era" and replaces the perhaps more familiar AD.

Second, another word of explanation. You will note that the second of the seven events has a date inscribed as ca. 250 BCE*. The asterisk attached to a number looks a little unusual. At the beginning of chapter 2, I explain the asterisk's function as signifying a date that is approximate, legendary, and a process.

Third, a word of appreciation. I want to thank Kendi Mohn and Amanda Henderson, two students at Brite Divinity School in Fort Worth, for their careful reading of the manuscript of this book. Their insightful feedback has been very helpful and has improved it considerably.

ABBREVIATIONS

General and Bible Versions

*	Used to designate a date as approximate, legendary, and a process	M	Matthew's special source
		NIV	New International Version (2011)
BCE	before the Common Era	$\mathfrak{P}^{46}$	Chester Beatty papyrus, with Gospels and Acts, 2nd to 3rd century
ca.	circa, approximately		
CE	Common Era		
cf.	compare	Q	*Quelle*, hypothetical sayings "source" used by Matthew and Luke
chap(s).	chapter(s)		
e.g.	for example		
esp.	especially	RSV	Revised Standard Version
et al.	and others	trans.	translator, translated by, translation
idem	the same; that is, by the same author		
		v(v).	verse(s)
L	Luke's special source		
LXX	Septuagint, Greek translation of Hebrew Bible		

Old Testament

Gen.	Genesis	Ezra	Ezra
Exod.	Exodus	Neh.	Nehemiah
Lev.	Leviticus	Esther	Esther
Num.	Numbers	Job	Job
Deut.	Deuteronomy	Ps(s).	Psalm(s)
Josh.	Joshua	Prov.	Proverbs
Judg.	Judges	Eccles.	Ecclesiastes
Ruth	Ruth	Song	Song of Songs
1–2 Sam.	1–2 Samuel	Isa.	Isaiah
1–2 Kings	1–2 Kings	Jer.	Jeremiah
1–2 Chron.	1–2 Chronicles	Lam.	Lamentations

Ezek.	Ezekiel	Mic.	Micah
Dan.	Daniel	Nah.	Nahum
Hosea	Hosea	Hab.	Habakkuk
Joel	Joel	Zeph.	Zephaniah
Amos	Amos	Hag.	Haggai
Obad.	Obadiah	Zech.	Zechariah
Jon.	Jonah	Mal.	Malachi

Apocryphal/Deuterocanonical Books

1–4 Macc.	1–4 Maccabees	Sir.	Sirach/Ecclesiasticus

New Testament

Matt.	Matthew	1–2 Thess.	1–2 Thessalonians
Mark	Mark	1–2 Tim.	1–2 Timothy
Luke	Luke	Titus	Titus
John	John	Philem.	Philemon
Acts	Acts	Heb.	Hebrews
Rom.	Romans	James	James
1–2 Cor.	1–2 Corinthians	1–2 Pet.	1–2 Peter
Gal.	Galatians	1–3 John	1–3 John
Eph.	Ephesians	Jude	Jude
Phil.	Philippians	Rev.	Revelation
Col.	Colossians		

Pseudepigrapha of the Old Testament

2 Bar.	2 Baruch	Pss. Sol.	Psalms of Solomon
1 En.	1 Enoch	T. Reu.	Testament of Reuben
Let. Aris.	Letter of Aristeas		

Dead Sea Scrolls

1QS	Serek Hayahad (Rule of the Community)

Ancient Sources

Appian
Mith. — Mithridates

Augustine
Civ. — De civitate Dei (City of God)

Cicero
Prov. cons. — De provinciis consularibus (Consular Provinces)

Quint. fratr. — Epistulae ad Quintum fratrem (Letters to Brother Quintus)

Rab. Perd. — Pro Rabirio Perduellionis Reo (For Rabirius on a Charge of Treason)

Verr. — In Verrem (Against Verres)

Diodorus Siculus
Hist.   Bibliotheca historica (His-
             torical Library)

Eusebius
Hist. eccl. Historia ecclesiastica (Eccle-
             siastical History)

Ignatius
Eph.   To the Ephesians

Irenaeus
Haer.   Adversus haereses (Against
             Heresies)

Josephus
Ant.   Jewish Antiquities
J.W.   Jewish War

Justin
Dial.   Dialogus cum Tryphone
             (Dialogue with Trypho)

Juvenal
Spect.   Spectacula (Spectacles)

Macrobius
Sat.   Saturnalia

Martial
Spect.   Spectacula (Spectacles)

Philo
Mos.   De vita Mosis (Life of
             Moses)

Pliny the Elder
Nat.   Naturalis historia (Natural
             History)

Plutarch
Alex.   Alexander
Caes.   Caesar

Seneca
Ben.   De beneficiis (Benefits)

Suetonius
Aug.   Divus Augustus
Cal.   Gaius Caligula

Tacitus
Ann.   Annales (Annals)
Hist.   Historiae (Histories)

INTRODUCTION

Seven Events

So what is this book about? Why should you bother reading it? Reading it because an instructor assigned it to you to read is not a bad reason. But is there any payoff? Good questions.

Here's the short answer: the seven chapters of this book provide an orientation to some important aspects of the early Jesus movement and the New Testament. Reading it will enlighten you about the beginnings of the Christian movement and help your understanding of the New Testament.

Here's the long answer: Seven hundred years. Seven chapters. Seven events or key dates. Three times seventy (or so) pages. This book does not pretend to be comprehensive. Rather it is transparently selective. Each chapter highlights a particular event. There are many, many other events that we could have highlighted. The selected events are of varying lengths; like a blind date gone bad, one even lasts a couple of hundred years!

What makes each event special? How were they selected? I take each event as a focal point for larger cultural dynamics and sociohistorical realities that were in some way significant for followers of Jesus and the New Testament. I use them as entry points, as launching pads, to talk about these significant and larger realities.

Chapters 1–4 highlight four key events in the time period prior to the emergence of the Jesus movement. Each event, though, leads us into cultural configurations that are crucial for the Jesus movement; so in each of these chapters we will also jump forward to the Jesus movement. Then in chapters 5–7 we center on three events of great consequence for the Jesus movement.

These key events recognize that the ancient world was multicultural. Though so much a feature of our worlds, multiculturalism did not come into existence in the last decade or so. The early Jesus movement emerges in a multicultural world. It is enmeshed in this world and negotiates it daily.

So in chapter 1 we consider the first key moment: 323 BCE, the year Alexander the Great died. That's over three hundred years before the time of Jesus. How much do we care about Alexander? Enough to review some of his major accomplishments so as to focus on his important legacy. He sets in motion forces that spread Greek language and Hellenistic culture across the ancient world. Hellenistic culture did not suddenly replace all other cultures but entangled itself with local cultures to create multicultural worlds. Jumping ahead three centuries, we look at some of the ways the early Jesus movement participates in some of these dynamics.

Why does that matter? Chapter 2 takes up one expression of the spread of Hellenistic culture: the translation of Jewish Scriptures from Hebrew into Greek. This *process*—and I will emphasize this dynamic—seems to be under way by around the 250s BCE. This translation, known as the Septuagint, was a way to negotiate a multicultural world. The Septuagint became the Scriptures of the early movement of Jesus-followers. So jumping ahead a couple of centuries, we look at how the Septuagint (the LXX) provides them with resources, language, and paradigms for understanding Jesus.

In chapter 3 we pick up another layer of cultural traditions. Part of this Greek-dominated, multicultural world comprised Jewish traditions and culture. We look at a major incident in which Hellenistic and Jewish traditions collide, and in which Jewish practices are defended and asserted—namely, when the Jerusalem temple is rededicated in 164 BCE. The villain is King Antiochus Epiphanes. The hero is the local boy Judas Maccabeus. We sketch out some of the key dynamics of this Jewish world and, jumping ahead, locate Jesus in this diverse and vibrant tradition.

In chapter 4 another major power player comes to the fore: Rome. In 63 BCE the Roman general Pompey establishes Roman control of Judea. Jewish folks negotiate Roman rule in various ways. Jumping ahead a century or so, we look at some of the diverse ways followers of Jesus, who was crucified by Rome and its Jerusalem allies, negotiate imperial power.

Chapters 5–7 focus specifically on three events of central significance for the Jesus movement emerging in this multicultural world. Chapter 5 focuses on Jesus's execution in 30 CE. Only bad boys were crucified in Rome's world. The chapter thinks about how King Jesus threatened the Roman order and how, thereafter, Jesus's followers make sense of this event.

Chapter 6 thinks about the emergence of the writings that will eventually make it into the New Testament. They are written in the window of about 50–130 CE. Chapter 7 develops the larger question of the processes by which the New Testament canon is formed and then ratified in 397 CE.

Seven hundred years of human experience. Seven chapters. Seven key events. Obviously that is selective. Obviously we leave out many other key events. The seven events function as entry points into the worlds that constitute the complex multicultural environment in which the Jesus movement emerges.

Dates and History?

People often think of studying history as the boring and tedious task of learning dates. Often studying history has focused on "Great Men" and their political and military exploits, ignoring women, common people, and everyday living and social structures. Often history has concentrated its efforts on discovering "what really happened." That's not the sort of history this book undertakes.

Yes, we do have seven key dates or events. Yes, we do have some "big names" and "Great Men." They don't come much bigger than Alexander the (not so?) Great, or Judas Maccabeus, or the Roman general Pompey and the emperors who follow him to power. But I'm not interested in them for their own sake. I'm not much interested in how many battles they won, or how they won them, or how much political power they had. I'm much more interested in the impact of their victories and their power on the little people, the common folks. Think of these key dates as being in the service of demographics or cultural dynamics.

Our focus is on the emergence of the early Jesus movement. This was not a movement that elites and "Great Men and Women" joined. Jesus came from a poor town in a country under Roman imperial power. He was an artisan. He died on a Roman cross. His followers, at least initially, constituted a movement of largely common folks who every day experienced varying degrees of poverty and powerlessness in a multicultural world. That is, this movement was not a superspiritual one that somehow escaped or ignored the socioeconomic realities of the time. They did not live ten feet above poverty, sickness, disease, food shortages, taxes, slavery, and hard work—the normal conditions of most poor folks living in the Roman Empire. They were enmeshed in this larger complex world whether they wanted to be or not. There was no escaping the consequences of what the small ruling elites of "Great Men and Women" did or how they structured the world for their own advantage.

Thus, instead of focusing on the powerful as though they are the whole story, one can do history from below, focusing on people and the social and cultural environments in which they lived. This people's-history perspective thinks about the impact of larger cultural movements and political structures on common folks.[1] In the ancient world, that is somewhat hard to do because most of the sources—though not all—come from elite males. They aren't much interested in nonelites. But our focus on the early Jesus movement takes us immediately into a group of common folks. By learning about their worlds and by reading their writings, we can gather some idea of how they negotiated this world of intertwining traditions: Greek culture, Jewish culture, and Roman imperial power.

The term "negotiated" is important. By "negotiated," I don't mean that someone brought donuts, or bagels and cream cheese with coffee, for a meeting where several parties try to hammer out deals that serve their own best interests. No such meeting is among our seven key events. I am using the term "negotiate" to refer to how they lived, how they made their way, in their complex world as followers of Jesus.

And I don't use "negotiate" to mean opposition. I am not suggesting that Jesus-followers automatically opposed Greek culture, Jewish practices, or Roman power. That is not so. There is no evidence for a singular approach of conflict or opposition or persecution. For much of our time period, most followers of Jesus did not need to worry about being thrown to lions because everyone hated them. That's a very inaccurate stereotype.

There is no doubt, though, that interactions were complex. In places there was some opposition. After all, followers of Jesus followed one who had been crucified by Rome and its allies. But there was also plenty of cultural imitation and accommodation. Christians drew resources such as language and ideas and social structures from each of these cultural streams. They wrote in Greek. They read Jewish Scriptures. They followed Jesus as members of his kingdom or *empire*, which they saw as eventually ruling over everything. They accommodated, they contested, they competed, they survived.

As strange as it might sound to us, the early Jesus group was a minority movement. It was initially very small, hardly a blip on the screen for most people. Living as a minority movement in a complex society is not easy. Powerlessness shapes your identity, your ways of being, your interactions with others, how you organize yourselves as a group, what you think and talk about, how others perceive you and interact with you. This minority status, of course, changes over the centuries. By the fourth century the Christian movement had

---

1. For a much more developed discussion of a people's-history approach to the early Jesus movement, see Richard A. Horsley, ed., *Christian Origins*, vol. 1 of *A People's History of Christianity*, ed. Denis R. Janz (Minneapolis: Fortress, 2005).

much more presence and influence, especially when the emperor Constantine took it under his wing around 313 CE (for better or for worse).

We can't engage all of this in the seven-chapter sketch that follows. But these are some of the issues and social dynamics that come to the fore in our people's-history approach. The seven key events help us see something of the dynamics of the emerging Jesus movement and help us understand the New Testament that those dynamics produced.

The Death of Alexander the Great
(323 BCE)

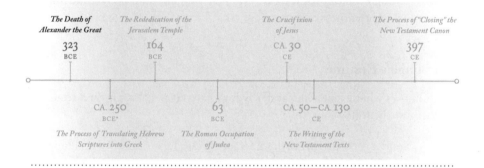

*H*e didn't tag himself Alexander the Great, but certainly history has come to know him as that. Two thousand years later he is still known as "the Great." He died on June 10, 323 BCE, only thirty-three years old. He was conqueror of much of the known world at an age when many of us have not yet figured out what we want to be when we grow up.

Was he really great? And why begin a book on the New Testament and the early Jesus movement with his death in 323 BCE? That's some three centuries before Jesus's ministry. There were no churches and no Jesus-followers in Alexander's time. With three centuries dividing them, what does Alexander have to do with Jesus and the early Jesus movement? That's the big question I want to think about in this chapter.

Alexander was an overachiever. He was king of Macedonia for thirteen years, from 336–323 BCE.[1] He conquered the world's leading superpower,

---

1. I use BCE to indicate "before the Common Era" and CE to indicate "Common Era."

Persia, and established an empire that stretched from Greece in the west, to India and Afghanistan in the east, and to Egypt in the south. He was a king, a general, a warrior, a world conqueror. He was also a party boy, a heavy drinker, bisexual, capable of violent temper tantrums, and paranoid.

Alexander casts a huge shadow. He's the sort of man of whom legends are born, in his own time and ever since. He has multiple personalities and a lengthy afterlife through the millennia. In our own time, Oliver Stone's movie *Alexander* (Warner Brothers, 2004) is a case in point. As with other key figures in history such as Jesus and Paul, it can be difficult to separate fact from legend and to figure out exactly what he was about. Will the real Alexander please stand up?

We'll start by outlining his kingly-soldierly career, next take up the question of why he might matter for the early Jesus movement, and then contemplate the notions of greatness and manliness that he was said to exemplify.[2]

Alexander's Résumé

Who knows what events Alexander would have chosen for his own résumé? I'll suggest the following:

- Alexander was born in northern Greece in late July of 356 BCE to Philip II, king of Macedonia, and his fourth wife, Olympias. Philip had unified Macedonia and led it in a resurgence of military, political, and economic power among the states of mainland Greece.
- But with Alexander nothing is simple or unambiguous, especially not his birth. Legends developed about his superhuman origins. One tradition claimed that his ancestors included the superhero Heracles, son of the

2. Helpful for this chapter have been E. Badian, "Alexander the Great and the Unity of Mankind," *Historia* 7 (1958): 425–44; Karl Galinsky, *Classical and Modern Interactions* (Austin: University of Texas Press, 1992), esp. "Multiculturalism in Greece and Rome," 116–53; A. B. Bosworth, *Alexander and the East: The Tragedy of Triumph* (Oxford: Clarendon, 1996); Diana Spencer, *The Roman Alexander: Reading a Cultural Myth* (Exeter, UK: University of Exeter Press, 2002); Waldemar Heckel and Lawrence A. Tritle, eds., *Crossroads of History: The Age of Alexander* (Claremont, CA: Regina Books, 2003); Joseph Roisman, ed., *Brill's Companion to Alexander the Great* (Leiden: Brill, 2003); Ian Worthington, ed., *Alexander the Great: A Reader* (London and New York: Routledge, 2003); Claude Mossé, *Alexander: Destiny and Myth* (Baltimore: Johns Hopkins University Press, 2004); Robin Lane Fox, *The Classical World: An Epic History from Homer to Hadrian* (New York: Basic Books, 2006); Peter Green, *The Hellenistic Age: A History* (New York: Modern Library, 2007); Waldemar Heckel and Lawrence A. Tritle, eds., *Alexander the Great: A New History* (Oxford: Wiley-Blackwell, 2009). For artwork, see Nikólaos Gialoúris et al., *The Search for Alexander: An Exhibition* (New York: New York Graphic Society, 1980–81).

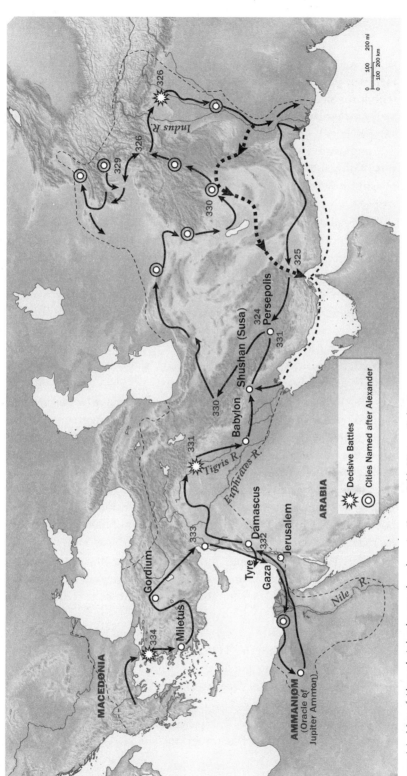

Figure 1.1. Map of Alexander's battles, travel, and empire (Source: Bible History Online)

supreme god Zeus, as well as Achilles, the military hero of the Trojan wars. Heracles was the ultimate strongman and model of macho masculinity (Diodorus Siculus, *Hist.* 17.1.5). Another tradition asserts that because a serpent was observed lying next to Alexander's mother, Olympias, Philip stopped having sex with her, thinking that her partner was a divine being. The implication is that Alexander's conception involved divine intervention (Plutarch, *Alex.* 2.4). Through his life, Alexander increasingly seems to claim a divine identity. Such legends present him as a superhero.

- As a youth, Alexander studies subjects such as philosophy, rhetoric, and geometry under the famous philosopher Aristotle. As a budding warrior, he learns war in his father's army against a coalition of Athenian and Theban armies.

- At the age of twenty in 336 BCE, Alexander becomes king after his father, Philip, is murdered. The murder is bad enough, but it happens, unfortunately, at his daughter's wedding. Why does his murder happen? Nothing is straightforward. One rumor has it that Alexander's mother incited the murder to ensure that Alexander becomes king. Another rumor attributes the assassination to the Persians, who fear Philip's imminent military campaign against them.

- Alexander inherits his father's plan to attack the Persian (or Achaemenid) Empire. Perhaps this plan avenges previous Persian aggression against Greek states. At least it seeks to free Greek cities in Asia Minor. Alexander seems to understand this to mean the conquest of the whole known world. This project will occupy him for the rest of his life. He does not sit at home and send his troops away on lengthy campaigns. Alexander literally leads his army and its support team (including philosophers, poets, scientists, and historians) across thousands of miles and into battle for the next eleven years. He does not return to Macedonia.

- In 334 BCE, his army, estimated to number some 30,000 foot soldiers (including archers and javelin throwers) and 5,000 cavalry, crosses from Macedonia into Asia Minor (modern Turkey) across the Hellespont, the narrow strip of water that divides Europe (the West) and Asia (the East).

- He wins several major battles over Persian forces, first at the Granicus River in northwest Asia Minor in 334 BCE, and then in 333 BCE at Issus, the crossroads of Asia Minor and northern Syria. The Persian king Darius III escapes, though Alexander captures Darius's mother, wife, and children.

- In 332–331 he heads south and gains control of Syria and Palestine. Egypt surrenders without a battle. He is proclaimed a pharaoh and son of the Egyptian god Osiris. In 331 he founds the city of Alexandria, which he

Figure 1.2. Sarcophagus with a depiction of Alexander fighting the Persians. (Wikimedia Commons)

names after himself and is one of numerous cities bearing his name. The city flourishes and, with Rome and Antioch in Syria, becomes one of the three largest cities of the Roman Empire.

- Southwest from Alexandria, he visits the famous oracle of Ammon (or Amun) at Siwah Oasis (in the desert of Egypt, near the present Libyan border). Legend has it that the oracle identifies him as the son of Zeus-Amun. Subsequently he seems to understand himself to be divine, an understanding that will become increasingly controversial. Being identified as divine was a way of recognizing his great power and rule and his great benefactions of material favors.

- Alexander marches his army over a thousand miles to the northeast, into the center of the Persian Empire. For a third time he battles Darius, and he wins at Gaugamela on the Tigris River in 331 BCE. Again Darius, who seems to have incredible good luck, escapes.

- In 330 BCE Alexander loots and burns the Persian capital, Persepolis. Darius escapes again, but this time his luck runs out. He is assassinated by one of his own officials. Alexander avenges the king's death by publicly executing the official, and he honors Darius by burying him in the tombs of the Persian kings. Alexander has gained great glory in defeating the mighty Persian Empire, dominant for over two hundred years. He now rules the Macedonian Empire. He tries to win Persian support by introducing Persians into his command structure. Alexander adopts Persian clothing and customs such as *proskynēsis*, a practice in which an inferior bows before a superior. Many Macedonians resist such practices. He executes some who are critical.

- During 330–327 he pacifies the eastern Persian Empire (eastern Iran) via much fighting.

- After marrying Roxana (Roxane/Roxanne), the beautiful daughter of a leading Persian, Alexander invades India. In 326 he defeats Porus, the rajah or king of Punjab in western India, at the Hydaspes River. Shortly afterward, his troops, wearied by and resentful of a campaign that never ends, revolt. They refuse to advance at the Hyphasis (now Beas) River. The thousands of miles of marching and of battle have taken their toll.

- The army turns back. By river, sea, and land, and with military actions along the way, Alexander heads westward to Susa, 160 miles east of the city of Babylon. At Susa in 324, Alexander organizes a mass, five-day wedding, Persian-style. Alexander marries two women, one of whom is Darius's oldest daughter, Stateira. Some ninety of his leading officers marry Persian women.

- The army again revolts in resentment against Alexander's attempts to include Persian troops. Alexander responds harshly in executing some of the leaders, and he increases the pay for loyal troops. At Opis on the Tigris River north of Babylon, he is also said to stage a sacrifice and banquet of reconciliation in 324, in which he prays for harmony between the Macedonians and Persians.

- Alexander plans to extend his empire south into Arabia. But in June of 323 BCE he becomes ill at Babylon, and he dies in the same year. Nothing is ever simple with Alexander. Did he get sick naturally (malaria?), or was he poisoned by one of his own men? Alexander's body is taken to Egypt, supposedly for burial at the Siwah Oasis, close to his "father" Zeus-Amun; instead he is entombed in Alexandria.

- Despite all his wives, Alexander leaves no adult heir. Power struggles break out among his generals, but none initially prevails. Some fifty or so years later, by the 270s BCE, three kingdoms emerge as successors to Alexander's empire and kingship until they give way before the next superpower: Rome. In one kingdom, Egypt, Ptolemy establishes a dynasty of kings (the Ptolemies) that lasts nearly three hundred years, until Cleopatra—yes, *that* Cleopatra—is defeated by the Roman Octavian in 31 BCE at the battle of Actium. Octavian becomes the first Roman emperor, known as Augustus. At its largest the second kingdom (of Alexander's legacy) spans western Turkey to Afghanistan and is centered in Syria. It is ruled by the Seleucid dynasty of kings. Through the centuries, it loses territory in the west and east until the Roman general Pompey conquers what is left in Syria in 64 BCE. The third kingdom, Macedonia itself, is strongly disputed until 276 BCE, when Antigonus Gonatas establishes the Antigonid dynasty of kings, which rules for over a hundred years until Rome defeats it in 168 BCE.

Alexander Is Dead: So What?

This is but one telling of Alexander's life. Since his own time there have been numerous retellings, numerous constructions of Alexander's identity. The outline above selectively highlights his military-kingly accomplishments in defeating the Persian Empire and in building the Macedonian Empire. It does not include numerous other aspects of his life: his wounds suffered in battle; the high value he placed on friendship; his active sex life with females and males (including his male lover Hephaestion, who died in 324); his polygamy (tradition records three wives and a lover); his heavy drinking; his legendary superhorse Bucephalas, after whom he named a city in India (Bucephalia); his quick temper; his cold-blooded murder of close supporters (Parmenion, Philotas, Cleitus, Callisthenes); his generous spirit; his growing paranoia; or his increasing assertions of his divinity and the resulting debates.

Through it all, what was Alexander trying to accomplish? How do we make sense of his activity and accomplishments? Historians have wrestled with these questions and offered explanations variously emphasizing cultural, economic, and political motives. Was he, for example, trying to civilize barbarians with superior Greek culture? Or was he trying to establish a cosmopolitan world with a fusion of Western and Eastern cultures, the unity of humankind, and the common fatherhood of Zeus? Was he a pragmatist who sought to use the expertise and skills of local people to enhance his own (Macedonian) interests? Was he looking to take over the land and wealth of the Persian Empire first through booty and plunder, and then by taxes and levies, or was he seeking new economic interactions through settlement, trade, and access to resources? Was he, as leader of all the Greek states, set on military revenge against Persia for age-old violations against Greek states? Did he inherit such a mission from his father, and then set out to outdo his father? Or was he a man with a political vision to rule the world? Was he a man who liked the companionship and conquest of war?

We cannot evaluate these options here. Alexander, clearly, was not a simple man, and simple explanations fail in the face of his complexities. Some of these options, though, are immediately less compelling than others. The proposals that center on grand, all-embracing intentions such as civilizing barbarians, fusing cultures, creating economic order, and imposing political visions seem less convincing. Better explanations run along the various lines of Alexander's personal quest for power, the satisfactions of contest and conquest (for whatever reasons), getting access to riches and resources from taxing Asia, and the pragmatic necessities of dealing with unfolding circumstances and negotiating competing and complex demands.

Spreading Hellenistic Culture

Whatever Alexander's aims or intentions, more important for our purposes is the question of the *impact* of his endeavors. We're back to that question: What does Alexander have to do with Jesus and Jesus-followers who live over three centuries after him?

A significant part of the answer has to do with the cultural forces that Alexander's military conquests let loose in the ancient world, forces that reverberated across thousands of miles and hundreds of years. Military conquest is never just about military victory and defeat; it is also about cultural influence and interaction. Whatever his intentions, Alexander's campaigns and armies, with their large supporting casts, set in motion the spread of Hellenistic culture throughout the territory he claimed.

Some historians have seen this process as the one-way spread of glorious Greek civilization over uncouth barbarians. No doubt some of the Macedonians thought like this, and it cannot be denied that Greek language and culture continued to be a major influence for centuries. But to see Alexander's impact as a one-way street is inadequate, partly because it ignores the local cultures that were in existence long before and after Alexander's time, and partly because it does not recognize that cultural interaction is a two-way street.

How did this spread of Hellenistic culture and its interaction with local cultures take place? Alexander's résumé highlights several ways that continued through the following centuries.

People Presence

Physical presence and interaction with local peoples were one means by which Hellenistic culture spread. It's impossible to march thousands of people through any geographical area without significant interactions with local people. Armies need food, shelter, supplies, equipment repairs, transportation, local knowledge, and recruits. The spread of Greek language, values, and practices, as well as the gaining of local knowledge, was inevitable as these personnel interacted with local peoples. Victories in battle not only establish control over territory, people, and resources; they are also coded with messages about cultural superiority and about more powerful gods. Religious syncretism resulted as local gods blended with Greek gods. In India, for example, post-Alexander statues of Buddha appeared presenting him like Apollo and wearing Greek clothing. Such people-to-people give-and-take would continue for centuries.

Local Alliances

Alexander also sought alliances with local peoples. He educated upper-status local young men in Greek language and ways. He included local Persian peoples in administering areas of his empire and admitted others to his army. He thereby utilized their skills and local knowledge while incorporating them into the sphere of Hellenistic culture. Intermarriages between Greeks and non-Greeks (Alexander married three local women) continued over subsequent centuries. Alexander's journeys and mapping of routes not only opened up new worlds, but also provided opportunities for trade to develop.

Urban Development

Establishing cities was another major means of cultural impact and exchange. Traditions attribute to Alexander the founding of more than seventy cities, a number of which were named after him, such as Alexandria in Egypt. The number is inflated, but the importance it attributes to cities is not. It is said that subsequently the Seleucid line of his successors founded an additional sixty cities. Some cities were military outposts; others were settled by Greek colonists and veterans, along with local peoples, with primarily administrative and commercial purposes. Whatever their intent, cities functioned as centers of Greek language, culture, and political structures. For example, city constitutions established a council, public officials, and elections. Cities included Greek features like the *agora*—both a political gathering space and a commercial marketplace—and theaters. Institutions proliferated, such as the gymnasium, which was not a health club or basketball center: it promoted physical and intellectual activity, making Greek myths, art, literature, ideas, and architecture accessible, along with training in rhetoric, a crucial skill for public leadership. The gymnasium maintained elite status by excluding those of lower status. It underlined Greek identity by requiring exercise in the nude, the norm among Greeks but not so among locals.

Such interactions continued for centuries. The influence of Greek language and culture was uneven and varied across the known world, both in terms of geography and levels of status. A local peasant farmer and village, operating largely as a self-sufficient subsistence economy, could perhaps get by somewhat untouched. But it was not so for others such as traders, craftsmen, merchants, and urban dwellers. Greek became a common language, and language always brings with it cultural values and practices.

Two-Way Traffic

The cultural traffic, though, went two ways. Greek language and culture did not sweep away all before it. It interacted with local cultures. Whether by ideology or pragmatism, Alexander had been receptive to Persian practices such as those relating to dress and the controversial *proskynēsis* (the kneeling of inferiors before a superior). His officers, though, were more resistant. Alexander was also open to Indian medical practices and philosophy. Reports indicate that one of Alexander's successors, Seleucus Nikator of Syria, made a peace treaty with the ruler of India, Chandragupta, and gives Chandragupta his daughter Cornelia in marriage to secure the alliance. The line of Ptolemies, the Greeks that ruled Egypt, was often presented in Egyptian dress as pharaohs. And some Greeks in Egypt adopted Egyptian religious practices. The Egyptian cult of Isis spread extensively, mingling with local religious expressions. As we will see in the next two chapters, some Jewish elites readily adopted Greek practices, others tried to reject them, and Jewish gatherings (synagogues) attracted non-Jewish participants.

For many people, as a result, a genuinely multicultural world resulted: some degree of cultural hybridization marked their existence. Xenophobia (fear of foreigners) attests such a world. The Roman orator Cicero knows for sure that Jews and Syrians are "born to be slaves" (*Prov. cons.* 10),[3] and that Africans, Spaniards, and Gauls are "uncouth and barbarous nations" (*Quint. fratr.* 1.1.27).[4] Yet Meleager of Gadara (late second to early first century BCE) celebrates his hybrid identity, while recognizing that a common humanity overrides local divisions. He outlines his hybridity—born in Gadara in Syria, lived in Tyre, and then the Greek island of Cos—and invites his readers to celebrate their own: "If you are a Syrian, *Salam!* If you are a Phoenician, *Naidius!* If you are a Greek, *Chaire!* And say the same yourself" (Meleager 7.419).[5] And what language does Meleager use to celebrate his

---

3. *Cicero*, trans. Walter Miller et al., 30 vols., Loeb Classical Library (Cambridge: Harvard University Press, 1913–2010).

4. Ibid.

5. *The Greek Anthology with an English Translation,* trans. W. R. Paton, 5 vols., Loeb Classical Library (Cambridge: Harvard University Press, 1916–18).

multicultural inclusivism and to invite his readers to recognize their common humanity? Greek, of course!

Alexander and Jesus

What do Alexander and this multicultural world that he significantly shapes have to do with Jesus three hundred years later? While Alexander is not single-handedly responsible for it, the world of Jesus and of the early Jesus movement reflects these processes that Alexander and his successors set in motion and sustained across the centuries.

Consider the following five features.

Language. Did Jesus speak Greek along with Aramaic? Some four hundred years after Alexander's death, early Jesus-followers write letters and accounts of Jesus's ministry to instruct and encourage one another. They do so in the common language of their multicultural world, Greek. And when they read their Scriptures—the Hebrew Bible—they do this in Greek as well, not in Hebrew, as we will see in the next chapter. That does not mean Greek obliterated all other languages: it didn't. But it does mean that, thanks to Alexander, Greek became the common language for many.

Cities. Cities are very important for the early Jesus movement. Paul addresses gatherings in cities such as Corinth, Thessalonica, and Philippi, the last two being in Alexander's Macedonia. In its narratives about mission journeys, the book of Acts focuses on cities. The book of Revelation addresses seven churches in cities in western Asia Minor (Rev. 2–3).

It would be nonsense to claim that Alexander invented cities in general or established all these particular cities and single-handedly paved the way for the Jesus movement: he did not. But by establishing cities, connecting them by roads and harbors, and enabling them to function as political, economic, and cultural centers, Alexander and his successors, including the Romans, underlined the importance of urban landscapes for significant human and cultural interaction. In cities, people found livelihood, community, allegiance, identity, security, cultural stimulation, economic prospects and deprivation, religious belonging, and revelation of divine purposes.

The New Testament documents reflect cultural interactions that happen in cities. Notice the vast array of nationalities and languages that Acts 2, the Pentecost scene, identifies as being present in Jerusalem: "And how is it that we hear, each of us, in our own native language? Parthians, Medes, Elamites, and residents of Mesopotamia, Judea and Cappadocia, Pontus and Asia, Phrygia and Pamphylia, Egypt and the parts of Libya belonging to Cyrene,

Figure 1.3. Theater at Ephesus (Norman Herr/Wikimedia)

and visitors from Rome, both Jews and proselytes, Cretans and Arabs—in our own languages we hear them speaking about God's deeds of power" (2:8–11). The account, of course, is written in Greek!

Later, Acts (19) narrates an incident in the city of Ephesus in which citizens assemble in a theater. There they assert their city's identity, defend the favor of the city's protector-goddess Artemis, declare their political allegiance, secure their sense of community and belonging, and guard their livelihoods against an outsider (Paul) who questions their religious practices and thereby threatens the city's existence. Jesus-believers in Corinth struggle with Paul over how Jesus-believers might engage these urban centers. Should they take one another to court (1 Cor. 6:1–11)? Should they eat food offered to idols (1 Cor. 8–11)? How should they conduct worship when houses in cities have areas that are regarded as public space (1 Cor. 12–14)?

Other New Testament writings locate various events in the *agora*. There children play, day laborers hope to be hired, status is asserted and honored, authorities maintain law and order, and religious and philosophical debates take place (Matt. 11:16; 20:3; 23:7; Acts 16:19; 17:17). Jails, temples, lawcourts, military barracks, houses, and streets figure as well. Cities were an important feature of this world in which the early Jesus movement got under way, and Jesus-believers did a lot of daily living in them.

PAUL AND ACTS:
WILL THE REAL PAUL PLEASE STAND UP?

As we will see in chapter 6, the seven letters that Paul probably wrote date from the decade of the 50s. In the book of Acts, Paul is the hero of the second half, increasingly from chapter 13 onward. But Acts was probably not written until about 100 CE or even later. Historians would talk about Paul's Letters as a primary source, while Acts would be a secondary source. That is, they would regard the Letters as a more historically reliable source.

Moreover, there are significant differences between the two sources in the presentation of Paul. In Acts, Paul does not write letters. Nor does he take a collection from the gentile churches for the church in Jerusalem, a very important matter for Paul. His gospel anticipating the return of Jesus to complete God's work fades. His concern with the manifestations of the gifts of the Spirit—a charismatic church structure—is replaced by a more institutional structure. In Acts, Paul's struggles over the law and conflicts with churches recede. There are conflicts between the Acts 15 account of the Jerusalem meeting and that of Galatians 2:1–10. It looks like the theological and pastoral agenda of the author of Acts shapes the presentation of Paul as the (almost) sole hero of the second part of Acts.

There surely are significant similarities. Yet we need to recognize that Acts is not giving us an eyewitness account but is offering an important interpretation of Paul.

Philosophical traditions. According to Acts 17:18, Paul debates with Stoic and Epicurean philosophers in Athens. Paul's own writings reflect some knowledge of Greek philosophical traditions. When he talks to the Corinthians about self-control in marriage (1 Cor. 7:5–9), he employs the notion of self-mastery prominent in Greek philosophical discourse. Two chapters later (9:24–27), he writes of runners in a race, running to win the prize after exercising self-control and disciplining their bodies. It is an image of Jesus-believers single-mindedly living for the goal of the completion of God's purposes. The image recalls the Isthmian games, which took place every two years just outside Corinth. To make his argument about faithful living, Paul also uses the common philosophical motif of the struggle or fight to live one's life appropriately.

Likewise, in several letters Paul includes lists of virtues and vices (Phil. 4:8–9; 1 Cor. 5:10–11; Gal. 5:19–23), showing his familiarity with a form of Greek philosophical speech that since Plato and Aristotle had elaborated desirable and undesirable ethical qualities. These Greek philosophical notions had infused popular culture—such as "low self-image" in pop psychology in our time. Paul uses this cultural knowledge to address his good news to Jesus-believers. He is a creature of his Greek-informed, multicultural world.

People of diverse ethnicities. From early on, Aramaic-speaking Jews and Greek-speaking people—Jews and gentiles—were part of the Jesus movement. The book of Acts records a group of believers called Hellenists (6:1). They were probably Jews who, though living in Jerusalem, had originally lived outside the land in the Diaspora, and for whom Greek was their main language. Not surprisingly, since conflict often accompanies cultural differences, Acts 6 indicates conflict between this group and "the Hebrews," who were probably speaking Aramaic, related to Hebrew. Subsequently Acts presents these Hellenists as playing a crucial role in spreading the Gospel to non-Jews (Acts 11:19–20).

The leading missionary among gentiles in the New Testament is Paul. He was a Greek-speaking, Diaspora Jew. Paul seems initially to have valued markers of distinctive Jewish identity like circumcision, Sabbath observance, and food purity. But after becoming a Jesus-believer, Paul reflects both his multicultural world and parts of his Jewish heritage in recognizing God as equally the God of all people (Jew and gentile).

Among the churches at Rome, for example, there were disputes between Jewish and gentile believers. Some Jewish believers wanted to maintain their particular ethnic identity amid cultural syncretism by observing the Sabbath and food purity. Others disagreed. In Romans 14–15 Paul argues that it doesn't matter whether Jesus-believers observe these practices. They can if they wish, just as gentile believers do not need to comply with them. There can be diverse practices along with their foundational unity in God's purposes of mercy for all people (Rom. 11:25–32). Paul spells out this theological understanding of God's mercy for all in the argument he presents in chapters 1–11 (e.g., 3:29–30). That is, as is appropriate to the multicultural forces at work in his world, Paul sees the communities of Jesus-believers as also being multicultural in membership and practice.

Religious experience. The story of Paul in Acts 17 shows us something of the religious dimensions of this world that Alexander helped to shape. Paul is in Athens, a great center of Hellenistic culture, and is distressed by its idols (17:16). Given the interactions of cultures, we can imagine representations of Greek gods such as Zeus and Hercules, as well as of non-Greek Eastern deities such as Isis or Serapis. Paul is accused, perhaps with a sneer by some, of being a preacher of "foreign divinities" (17:18). His point of engagement is to commend his Athenian listeners on their religious observance, then seek to reveal to them the identity of "an unknown god," for whom they have an altar (17:23).

Paul's reference to this altar to an unknown god tells us a lot. Its existence indicates that this is a world of many gods. Polytheism is (mostly) tolerant. It's also a world in which gods are commonly represented with images (idols) and honored with sacrifices, offerings, prayers, and meals. There is clearly considerable awareness of the impact of divine powers on daily life and a concern to cover all the bases with offerings and prayers. Religious practices such as sacrifices, offerings, prayers, and meals sought divine favors: good health, economic survival, love, revenge, business success, safe travel, and so forth. People took their blessings where they could find them, and they didn't want to alienate a power unknowingly.

Socially, people found in religious practices and affiliations a common identity and sense of community with other people in a culturally diverse and interactive world. Religious practices provided people with a way to make sense and meaning of a complex world, where life was often experienced by many to be harsh, frightening, and unpredictable. Religious practices thus offered resources for daily life. They offered the possibility of divine interventions that could transform adversity into favor, and of divine revelations that could offer direction and provide meaning.

In this supermarket of numerous religious expressions, the Paul of Acts fashions a message that speaks to this context. As is appropriate to this multicultural world, he proclaims a God who made all nations (17:26). His proclamation underlines a common humanity in the midst of religious and ethnic diversity. As is appropriate to the yearning for contact with the divine world, Paul proclaims a God who is nearby and not elusive (17:27–28). In quoting first the poet Epimenides ("In him we live and move and have our being") and then the Stoic philosopher Aratus ("We are his offspring"), he shows compatibility between his proclamation and Hellenistic traditions. His citation of Epimenides underlines God's accessibility; quoting Aratus asserts a common identity in which all people are "offspring," or children, of God. Both claims look to secure human community in a diverse and multifaceted world, as does Paul's assertion that "all people everywhere" are accountable to this God (17:30–31).

The early Jesus movement addressed these same experiences in other ways. Stories of Jesus as a healer and miracle worker presented him as one who is able to counter the debilitating damage of daily life. Stories of Jesus as an exorcist offered protection from hostile cosmic powers. Stories of Jesus as a teacher provided guidance in how to live. Accounts of Jesus as revealing the presence and future of God's reign or empire promised power and transformation in difficult circumstances and solicited allegiance to the one who has ultimate power. Stories of Jesus's welcoming marginalized and alienated people to eat with him offered food and welcoming community to those who struggled for both.

Paul presents his message as good news for troubled circumstances. It reveals God's powerful justice at work in transforming the world (Rom. 1:16–17). Paul offers a vision of a community in which the fundamental differences of ethnicity, status, and gender—markers of power and powerlessness—no longer define identity or exclude people: "There is no longer Jew or Greek, there is no longer slave or free, there is no longer male and female; for all of you are one in Christ Jesus" (Gal. 3:28). Among such communities were expressions of God's Spirit that empowered members to support one another (1 Cor. 12–14). And one can only imagine the reassuring and liberating good news of the declaration that, at the heart of the world, there are not hostile cosmic powers out to harm people, but a God whose loving power cannot be deflected or overcome by anything: "If God is for us, who is against us? . . . Who will separate us from the love of Christ? Will hardship, or distress, or persecution, or famine, or nakedness, or peril, or sword? . . . For I am convinced that neither death, nor life, nor angels, nor rulers, nor things present, nor things to come, nor powers, nor height, nor depth, nor anything else in all creation, will be able to separate us from the love of God in Christ Jesus our Lord" (Rom. 8:31, 35, 38–39).

Greek language. Cities. Philosophical traditions. People of diverse ethnicities. Religious experiences. Alexander didn't create this world intentionally or all by himself. Whatever his intentions, he and his successors let loose cultural forces that by the first century CE had shaped a world in which Greek language and ways had a dominant place, but also a world that through interaction with local cultures was multicultural. It offered a buffet of religious options in which people might find resources and meaning. We find the early Jesus movement located among such options and addressing the contours of its world.

Alexander the Great or the Not So Great?

There is one more aspect of Alexander's legacy to explore briefly. Was Alexander great? It's not hard to catalog some incredible accomplishments: his massive journeys, his numerous victories (at times with brilliant military strategy), his vast empire, his stimulation of trade and economic exchange, the spread of monarchies after his death, and the impact over subsequent centuries of Greek language, culture, and education—all by his thirty-third birthday. Impressive.

But in the not-so-great column are other factors. He was a skilled general, but his army mutinied against him several times. He was at times reckless in his own fighting, risking his own life, not a smart strategy for the army's commander! The price of his glory was the slaughter of tens of thousands of his own soldiers as well as of local peoples. That's a lot of misery for parents, siblings, children, villages, and towns. Local resources were co-opted and local communities and cultures disrupted. While he seemed to thrive on conquering people, as a king he paid much less attention to providing social order through administering his empire. He also failed to provide an heir: thus at his death his empire imploded from power struggles. In terms of character, his megalomania, his love for military glory, his obsession with his own divinity, his excessive drinking, and his paranoid and hot-tempered actions against "friends"—all these are part of the record.

But however we assess the man historically, there is no doubt that by the first century CE, the time of the early Jesus movement, Alexander has become a myth. He is a macho man, an action figure. This is not a matter of biology but of understanding masculinity. He was not Alexander the Sensitive or Alexander the Gentle: he was Alexander the Great.

What does this mean? In a male-dominated society, he defines male greatness by his manly actions of rule and courage. Not surprisingly, elite males want to be like Alexander, especially Romans and provincial elites who, like Alexander, have an empire to rule. Alexander provided a model for such men (and for powerful women) to secure their glorious place in the world by rule and courage. They could display their status, wealth, and power through mastery over others by involvement in government, military activity, civic benefaction, and personal patronage. Being like Alexander meant acting like Alexander, presenting oneself as a larger-than-life personality, with outstanding accomplishments of power, and of course a stage so that others could observe the spectacle. Being like Alexander meant actions that displayed and enhanced charisma, popularity, courage, divine favor, and military victory. Being like Alexander meant performing such actions for the good of others, but especially to secure one's position over others.

Lots of Roman men modeled themselves on Alexander. As we will see in chapter 4, the Roman general Pompey is an action figure. He conquers extensive territory in the East. That was Alexander's former stomping ground, so connections between Pompey and Alexander were inevitable. Like Alexander, he establishes cities and names them after himself, such as Pompeiopolis in Cilicia. That's downright pompous. Emulating Alexander as world conqueror, he becomes known as Pompey the Great. Accordingly, he celebrates his triumph or victor's parade in Rome in 61 BCE wearing, so it was claimed (and who knows?), one of Alexander's cloaks, thereby joining his own accomplishments with Alexander's conquering glory (Appian, *Roman History, Mith.* 1.117).

Julius Caesar (d. 44 BCE) is said to have read a biography of Alexander. He is reported to have been concerned that he (Julius Caesar) had not achieved nearly as much domination over so many people as Alexander had (Plutarch, *Caes.* 11.5–6). Not surprisingly, the biographer Plutarch pairs Caesar with Alexander and heightens the link between them.

Octavian, who became the emperor Augustus, conquered Alexandria. He paid homage at Alexander's tomb in 30 BCE (Suetonius, *Aug.* 18) and added an image of Alexander to his personal seal. Octavian designed his own tomb or mausoleum in Rome (which you can see in Rome to this day) to be like Alexander's.

The emperor Caligula (37–41 CE) imagined that he wore the armor of Alexander (Suetonius, *Cal.* 52). Brazenly (in an Alexanderesque manner?), he celebrated victory *before* his military campaign. The emperor Trajan (98–117 CE), after his Parthian war and campaigns through "Alexander's territory" in Mesopotamia, boasted that he had traveled farther than Alexander. Several emperors associated themselves with Alexander through his legendary horse, Bucephalas. Augustus honored the death of his own horse with a funeral mound (Pliny the Elder, *Nat.* 8.154–155), while Caligula nominated his own horse, named Incitatus, as consul and priest (Suetonius, *Cal.* 55).

This manly image was not the only image of Alexander. Other traditions constructed his manliness negatively by criticizing his murderous treatment of his friends, his despotic power, and his plunder of the nations (cf. Seneca, *Ben.* 1.13.1–3). But to the fore in these self-presentations is Alexander, the manly man, who personifies manliness and greatness in terms of power over others, military might and courage, imperial grandeur, world rule, self-interest, and political supremacy.

In the light of this construction of Alexander as a manly man, we think about how the New Testament writers present Jesus as a man. Not surprisingly as a reflection of the cultural worlds from which the writings originate, we have presentations of Jesus that highlight his great power. The Gospels, for example, present him as ruling over diseases, demons, the sea, wine and food, and sin (forgiveness). He has followers (disciples) who give him their allegiance. Jesus is not restricted by anything: he even rules over death and imperial power, since Rome and its Jerusalem allies cannot keep him dead.

Paul offers a similar comprehensive vision of the almost-supreme, cosmic power of Jesus as agent of God's purposes: "Then comes the end, when he hands over the kingdom to God the Father, after he has destroyed every ruler and every authority and power. For he must reign until he has put all his enemies under his feet. The last enemy to be destroyed is death. . . . When all things are subjected to him, then the Son himself will also be subjected to the one who put all things in subjection under him, so that God may be all in all" (1 Cor. 15:24–28). In this presentation, Jesus imitates yet out-alexanders Alexander and the Roman emperors. He outpowers them. He outrules them. In many ways, this presentation of Jesus as the man with great power who rules everything imitates and competes with the presentation of manliness that we have seen with Alexander, the world conqueror.

But that is not the whole picture. Paul certainly echoes the supreme power of imperial manliness in a letter interestingly written to Jesus-believers in the city of Philippi located in Macedonia in northern Greece, a city that Alexander's father, Philip, named after himself. Paul declares that God highly exalted Jesus and "gave him the name that is above every name, so that at the name of Jesus every knee should bend, in heaven and on earth and under the earth" (Phil. 2:9–10). Yet Paul borrows another image from his society to claim that Jesus did a decidedly *unmanly* thing first. Paul images Jesus as a slave. Slaves were the complete opposite of dominating, manly men. They were dominated, submissive, mastered by their masters, victims of imperial power. So Paul says that Jesus, instead of dominating others, "emptied himself, taking the form of a slave. . . . And being found in human form, he humbled himself and became obedient to the point of death—even death on a cross" (Phil. 2:7–8).

These actions are the exact opposite of Alexander's actions as a manly man. Paul offers a partially different vision of being a man and a human being. Along with dominating others, Jesus shows concern for the other in self-giving. Jesus's action of becoming a slave—the lowest of the low in the Greek and Roman worlds—exemplifies Paul's instruction about how Jesus-followers are to live: "Do nothing from selfish ambition or conceit, but in humility regard others as better than yourselves. Let each of you look not to your own interests, but to the interests of others" (Phil. 2:3–4). In Paul's presentation, Jesus's manly power over others exists alongside his unmanly self-emptying in becoming a slave, and in the ultimate act of providing benefit to others by giving his life.

Matthew's Jesus draws a similar contrast. He knows about the manly men of his age. His followers are not to imitate them. While "the rulers of the Gentiles lord it over" people, and "their great ones [think Alexander, Pompey, Augustus, and the rest of the Roman emperors] are tyrants over them," Jesus's followers are to renounce domination in favor of serving with life-giving actions, just as Jesus did (Matt. 20:24–28). They are to be like Jesus, not like Alexander.

Of course the "great men" would protest by saying that they do their noble actions for the benefit of others—and they have a good point that can't be denied. Many others *do* benefit from their actions of civic benefaction and personal patronage. And Matthew's Jesus does not contest this claim. Rather, he focuses attention on the fundamentally self-serving dynamic at work in being like Alexander. He declares an ultimate test for manly actions: to give one's life for many.

Why is this the test for manliness? How does one ace this test? It's simple though all-consuming. If one gives one's life, only the other is left to benefit. That's what Matthew's Jesus calls manly.

Things get complicated when Alexander and Jesus get together.

The Process of Translating Hebrew Scriptures into Greek
(ca. 250 BCE*)

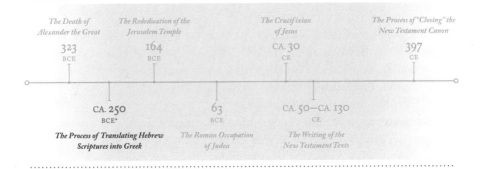

The Death of Alexander the Great
323 BCE

The Rededication of the Jerusalem Temple
164 BCE

The Crucifixion of Jesus
CA. 30 CE

The Process of "Closing" the New Testament Canon
397 CE

CA. 250 BCE*
The Process of Translating Hebrew Scriptures into Greek

63 BCE
The Roman Occupation of Judea

CA. 50–CA. 130 CE
The Writing of the New Testament Texts

*I*t would seem the most natural thing to expect. In the ancient world a Jewish person listening to the Jewish Scriptures read aloud (remember, most folks have limited literacy skills) would hear them in Hebrew. Jewish Scriptures, Hebrew language. Surely.[1]

---

1. Bibliography for this chapter includes Sidney Jellicoe, *The Septuagint and Modern Study* (Oxford: Clarendon, 1968); V. Tcherikover, "The Ideology of the Letter of Aristeas," in *Studies in the Septuagint: Origins, Recensions, and Interpretations*, ed. Sidney Jellicoe (New York: Ktav, 1974), 181–207; Rowan Greer, "The Christian Bible and Its Interpretation," in *Early Biblical Interpretation*, by James Kugel and Rowan Greer (Philadelphia: Westminster, 1986); Mogens Müller, *The First Bible of the Church: A Plea for the Septuagint*, Journal for the Study of the Old Testament: Supplement Series 206 (Sheffield: Sheffield Academic Press, 1996); Natalio Fernández Marcos, *Septuagint in Context: Introduction to the Greek Version of the Bible* (Leiden and Boston: Brill, 2000); Karen Jobes and Moisés Silva, *Invitation to the Septuagint* (Grand Rapids: Baker Academic, 2000); Albert Sundberg Jr., "The Septuagint: The Bible of Hellenistic Judaism," in *The Canon Debate*, ed. Lee Martin McDonald and James A. Sanders (Peabody, MA: Hendrickson, 2002), 68–90; Craig A. Evans, "The Scriptures of Jesus and His Earliest Followers," in McDonald and Sanders, *The Canon Debate*, 185–95; R. Timothy McLay, *The Use of the Septuagint in*

But not so.

We can't forget 'Xander the (Not So?) Great and the spread of Greek culture and language that he and his successors set in motion. Alexander changed things. One consequence—Jewish Scriptures, *Greek* language.

Though he is long dead, Alexander casts a long shadow. He left folks of various nationalities with a dilemma that they would wrestle with for centuries to come: How shall they make their way in this multicultural world dominated by Greek, or Hellenistic, culture?

Ignoring Greek culture wasn't really an option. Some fought it, others joined it. Many straddled it with a foot in several cultures, appropriating some dimensions but not others. But no one could ignore it.

Among various strategies, translating sacred writings into Greek was a way some Jewish folks adapted to this context while protecting a tradition and identity that were important to them.

This Greek translation of the Hebrew sacred writings came to be known eventually as the Septuagint, or LXX. Note the mix of cultures: Hebrew Scriptures translated into Greek, with a Latin name and Roman numerals. It's a complicated world.

Jewish Scriptures. *Greek* language.

This translation became the Scriptures of the early Jesus movement. How did that happen? When? And why? It did not just mean that some Jewish folks had forgotten how to speak Hebrew (though that's in the mix). Rather, the translation of Hebrew Scriptures into Greek is part of a larger issue of people of a minority tradition making and marking their way in a multicultural world dominated by Greek culture.

Sorting Out a Date

When did this translation happen? The date in the chapter title *seems* to suggest a clear answer—around the 250s BCE* or so. Alexander died in 323 BCE, so, doing the math, after some eighty or so years of cultural interactions, the translation from Hebrew to Greek takes place.

But we wouldn't need a whole chapter if things were that simple. You'll notice immediately the "ca." in front of 250 BCE. That ca. is an abbreviation for a Latin word *circa*, which means "about" or "around." So ca. 250 indicates an approximate date, about or around the 250s. You'll also notice that

---

New Testament Research (Grand Rapids: Eerdmans, 2003); Lee Martin McDonald, *The Biblical Canon: Its Origin, Transmission, and Authority* (Peabody, MA: Hendrickson, 2007). Clearly this introductory chapter can engage only a few of the multiple issues.

an asterisk (*) follows the numbers, ca. 250 BCE*. The asterisk—which we'll keep using—signifies two important things to keep in mind about this date.

First, the asterisk signifies that the ca. 250 BCE* date is a *legendary* date. That means we don't know for sure when translation of Jewish sacred writings from Hebrew into Greek began. But there is a legend or story in a Jewish writing called the *Letter of Aristeas* that sets the translation in the time period around the 250s BCE or so. We will look at this legend in a moment. The asterisk in the date signifies that the legend claims translation happened in about the 250s BCE, while at the same time recognizing that the time period in which the story sets this event is not (entirely?) historically reliable.

Second, the asterisk signifies that the ca. 250 BCE* date is a *process* date. The translation of the Hebrew writings into Greek did not happen at one time. It was not an effort coordinated by a committee or person. The canon of Hebrew Scriptures was fluid and not yet fixed. And the translation of

PROCESS OF TRANSLATION INTO GREEK

We see evidence of this translation process if we fast-forward a hundred years to another Jewish document, the *Wisdom of Ben Sira* (or *Sirach*). This document, found in the Apocrypha, is a collection of teaching attributed to Sirach and originally written in Hebrew. His grandson translates it into Greek in the year 132 BCE. He says this about translation:

> For what was originally expressed in Hebrew does not have exactly the same sense when translated into another language. Not only this book, but even the Law itself, the Prophecies, and the rest of the books differ not a little when read in the original.
>
> Prologue to Sirach

This is an important statement. In a writing dating to around 132 BCE, the grandson refers to three sections of Hebrew Scriptures—the Law (the Pentateuch or first five books), the Prophecies, and "the rest of the books." He notes that all of them, not just the Pentateuch, have now been translated into Greek. And, a little defensively, he recognizes that they don't have "exactly the same sense when translated into another language." Perhaps in this statement he reflects and deflects some criticism of translating Hebrew sacred writings into Greek. Translation always involves interpretation, and perhaps some people did not like it. And in presenting his own translation of his grandfather's teaching, Sirach's grandson keeps the process going by adding another translated book to the collection.

Hebrew Scriptures into Greek was open-ended in that it took place over many decades. The legend that dates this translation to around the 250s BCE* concerns only the translation of the Law, the first five books or Pentateuch of the Hebrew Scriptures. Translation of the prophetic books and the rest of the writings followed over the next century or so. Strictly speaking, "Septuagint" refers to the Pentateuch's translation into Greek, but the name has come to refer to the translation of all Hebrew Scriptures into Greek. I will use it in both senses.

As a result of this piecemeal effort over a lengthy period of time, there is considerable variety of style in the translations of the various Hebrew writings into Greek. Some are fairly literal, others are more free (e.g., Daniel, Job). Others have considerable discrepancies between the Hebrew and Greek versions. The Greek translation of Jeremiah, for example, is shorter than the Hebrew version, and has a different order. This unevenness indicates translation by different people over a lengthy period of time. So our ca. 250 BCE* date is an approximate date, a legendary date, and a process date.

We begin with the legend and its significance as a way in which some Jewish folks living outside the land of Judea in the Diaspora expressed their identity in a culturally complex world. Then we will look at why this date matters for the early Jesus movement. Keep in mind that notion of translation as a way of expressing and protecting one's identity in a multicultural world dominated by Greek culture.

The Origins of the Septuagint: The *Letter of Aristeas*

Our legend or story about the translation of the Pentateuch into Greek comes from a document called the *Letter of Aristeas*. This document, written in Greek (of course!), can be found in a collection of writings called the Old Testament Pseudepigrapha.[2] Dating the *Letter of Aristeas* is very difficult.

The story it tells is set in the time of Ptolemy II Philadelphus, the king of Egypt who reigned from 285 BCE to 247 BCE. But a story's setting is not necessarily the same as its time of writing. For reasons I will outline shortly, the *Letter of Aristeas* was written sometime after King Ptolemy's reign. Most scholars tend to date it sometime in the 100s BCE. Most locate its writing in Alexander's special city of Alexandria in Egypt.

The *Letter of Aristeas* presents itself as a letter or report written by Aristeas to his brother Philocrates, describing how the Jewish law (the Pentateuch, or

2. R. Shutt, trans., "Letter of Aristeas," in *The Old Testament Pseudepigrapha*, ed. James H. Charlesworth, 2 vols. (Garden City, NY: Doubleday, 1983–85), 2:7–34.

In a little more detail, with references to the *Letter of Aristeas*, here's the backstory:

- Verses 1–8: Aristeas introduces the story to his brother Philocrates, who is presented as someone who loves learning.
- Verses 9–11: The Egyptian king Ptolemy II Philadelphus (285–247 BCE) commissions the royal librarian Demetrios to collect all the books of the world. Demetrios suggests including the Jewish Law, but it must be translated into Greek. The king orders a letter to be sent to the Jewish high priest in Jerusalem, Eleazar, asking for assistance.
- Verses 12–27: Aristeas takes this receptivity to translating the Jewish Law into Greek as an opportunity to make a request. He asks that the king release Jewish slaves or prisoners whom the king's father brought to Egypt. The king magnanimously consents.
- Verses 28–32: The narrative returns to the translation issue. Demetrios suggests that the king write to the high priest in Jerusalem, requesting that he send six educated and virtuous men from each of the twelve tribes to undertake the translation.
- Verses 33–50: The king's letter to Eleazar the high priest in Jerusalem making this request is included, along with Eleazar's reply, celebrating the invitation and naming the seventy-two translators or elders.
- Verses 51–82: King Ptolemy chooses generous and high-quality gifts for Eleazar.
- Verses 83–120: Journeying to Judea with the gifts, Aristeas describes the wonderful land, the Jerusalem temple, and its priestly activity.
- Verses 121–72: Eleazar selects men of high personal and intellectual quality, competent in Greek and Hebrew, six from each of the twelve tribes. He elaborates the significance of the law and sends the elders/translators to King Ptolemy II with gifts.
- Verses 173–81: The seventy-two translators arrive in Alexandria to a warm welcome from the king, who bows seven times before the sacred Hebrew scrolls.
- Verses 182–300: For seven days, the king hosts welcoming banquets and engages in philosophical and ethical discussion with the translators.
- Verses 301–7: Demetrios the royal librarian escorts the translators to a nearby island to do their translating work. They accomplish their translation into Greek in seventy-two days.
- Verses 308–22: The translation of the Pentateuch is read first to the Alexandrian Jewish community and then to the king. It is received very positively.

first five books, Genesis to Deuteronomy) was translated from Hebrew into Greek. Aristeas narrates how the king of Egypt, Ptolemy, wants a copy of all the books in the world for his library in Alexandria, to make it a leading city of Greek culture. The librarian Demetrios (or Demetrius) thinks the collection should include the Jewish Law translated from Hebrew into Greek. Subsequently seventy-two learned scribes or scholars come from Jerusalem, sent by the chief priest Eleazar, to do the translation. Their translation for the library is greeted with much celebration by the Jewish people and by King Ptolemy in Alexandria.

A Legend, Not a Historical Report

While Aristeas sets his interesting story in the time of Ptolemy II's reign (285–247 BCE), there are problems with the historical accuracy of his account that suggest its legendary quality. While Ptolemy was a real king, Aristeas has it all wrong concerning Demetrios, whom he presents as the royal librarian. There was a historical Demetrios, yet he was associated not with King Ptolemy II Philadelphus, but with his father, Ptolemy I Soter (367–283 BCE). Ptolemy I was a Greek who had been one of Alexander's officers and successors and who had founded the Ptolemaic line of kings ruling Egypt after Alexander's death. In fact, Demetrios did not play well with the second Ptolemy, who sent him into exile. Demetrios died soon afterward. And a very big problem for the historical accuracy of Aristeas's scenario is that Demetrios was never the royal librarian of the library at Alexandria.

Also a big problem is that in several places Aristeas seems to draw material from the Septuagint translation itself. When he describes the gift of a table that King Ptolemy sends to the high priest Eleazar in Jerusalem, he seems to base it on the Greek translation of Exodus 25:23–30 (Let. Aris. 52–72). And when he describes the high priest's garments in the Jerusalem temple, he seems to base it on the Greek translation of Exodus 28–29 (Let. Aris. 96–99). What's wrong with that? The problem, of course, is that according to Aristeas's own narrative, these gifts are given *before* the translation is made. He seems to have gotten the cart before the horse.

Yet some scholars think that, while generally Aristeas's account is not a historical report, it may well contain some reliable historical information about the origins of the Septuagint translation. For example, it may be accurate in locating the translation's origin in the major cultural center of Alexandria, albeit in different circumstances. It may accurately identify the Pentateuch as the first part to be translated in a longer, ongoing process. And it may be right in recording assistance from Jerusalem.

Yet despite its lack of general historical accuracy, the *Letter of Aristeas* tells us important things about the significance of this Greek translation of the Hebrew Scriptures as a way in which Jewish folks modified and protected their identity, and thereby negotiated a complex, multicultural world dominated by Greek culture.

Jews and Gentiles Getting Together

Aristeas's account is not neutral. Its writer is very enthusiastic about this Greek translation of the Pentateuch. What's he selling? And why is it so important?

The *Letter* is very concerned with the interaction between Jews and non-Jews, or gentiles. Both gentiles and Jews are presented very positively. How do the two groups interact?

Gentiles Behaving Nicely

As representatives of Greek culture, King Ptolemy and Demetrios the librarian are enthusiastic about culture in general (*Let. Aris.* 124, 321). They are collecting all the books in the world for the Alexandrian library (*Let. Aris.* 9). Demetrios's suggestion to include a translation of the Pentateuch—which the king actively pursues (*Let. Aris.* 9–11, 29–32, 38–40)—accords these Jewish writings an honorable place among the world's literature. Demetrios and the king appear open to Jewish culture and affirming of it.

In the story, Aristeas the storyteller presents himself as a member of the king's court and a gentile, like King Ptolemy and Demetrios. Aristeas uses his power and position to request that the king release Jews who are in slavery in Egypt. As their ally, Aristeas argues that to honor the Jews by translating their writings into Greek requires equally dignified treatment of them as people. Arguing along theological lines, he points out to the king that "the same God who appointed them their Law prospers *your* kingdom" (*Let. Aris.* 15). Aristeas argues that all people worship the same God, though this God is known by different names. Jewish people "worship God . . . the creator of all, whom all people worship including ourselves, O King, except that we have a different name, . . . Zeus and Jove" (*Let. Aris.* 16).

Aristeas also presents himself as a believer in this Jewish God. He offers "hearty prayer to God to dispose [the king's] mind" to release the Jewish slaves (*Let. Aris.* 17). God listens to righteous gentiles like Aristeas. His prayer is answered, and the king's good-guy image is enhanced as he grants Aristeas's request (*Let. Aris.* 12–27, 35–37). The king says he wants to "grant favors . . . to all the Jews throughout the world" (*Let. Aris.* 38); he is a man of piety and benevolence and a man of his word.

Figure 2.1. Ptolemy II (Marie-Lan Nguyen/Wikimedia Commons)

Interestingly, King Ptolemy also says he releases the Jewish prisoners as "a thank offering to the Most High God, who has preserved the kingdom in peace and in highest renown" (*Let. Aris.* 37). The high priest Eleazar in Jerusalem attests the king's "piety toward our God" (*Let. Aris.* 42) and friendship and blessings toward Jewish people (*Let. Aris.* 44–45). He prays that "God the ruler of all should preserve your kingdom in peace" (*Let. Aris.* 45).

Accordingly, King Ptolemy generously sends Eleazar, the Jerusalem high priest, high-quality gifts (*Let. Aris.* 40–42, 51–82). Ptolemy personally supervises their construction (*Let. Aris.* 81). He warmly greets the seventy-two translators that come from Jerusalem to Alexandria (*Let. Aris.* 174–175). The king prostrates himself before the Hebrew scrolls seven times, thanking God, "whose oracles these are" (*Let. Aris.* 177–178). He declares an annual holiday in honor of these "men of God" (*Let. Aris.* 179–180), hosts them with fine accommodations and food prepared according to their customs (*Let. Aris.* 182–186), and engages them in conversation about philosophical matters for seven days (*Let. Aris.* 187–300). When the translation is completed, the king becomes chief cheerleader in preserving it and honoring the translators as "men of culture" (*Let. Aris.* 312–321).

King Ptolemy, along with Demetrios and Aristeas, is presented as a gentile who honors Israel's God and Jewish sacred writings, culture, and personnel.

Jews Behaving Nicely

And the Jewish characters in the story? The *Letter of Aristeas* presents the Jewish characters as similarly international in their outlook. They are open to and receptive of interaction with these gentiles and Greek culture. As we have noticed previously, Israel's God is presented as blessing King Ptolemy's rule and Egyptian kingdom, and as being worshiped among various peoples by different names. Yet God also looks out for the welfare of the king's Jewish prisoners, answering Aristeas's prayer to free them (*Let. Aris.* 20).

Eleazar, the high priest in Jerusalem, welcomes the king's proposal to translate the Hebrew writings into Greek (*Let. Aris.* 41–51). The men he chooses to do the translation—six from each of the twelve tribes, thereby representing the whole nation—are similarly open to Greek matters. They are educated in Jewish *and* Greek literature (*Let. Aris.* 121–127). Eleazar interprets the teaching of the law as symbols whose meaning is available to everybody, not just to Jews. Its teaching sustains a life that remembers God and is lived out in good actions (*Let. Aris.* 150–157). The seventy-two translators do not hesitate to travel to Egypt with the Hebrew scrolls (*Let. Aris.* 172, 176). They engage in seven days of feasting and conversation with the king (*Let. Aris.* 182–300). They talk Greek philosophy and ethics, engaging topics like good government (*Let. Aris.* 187–235), gaining wisdom (*Let. Aris.* 236–247), and living virtuous lives (*Let. Aris.* 248–294). The seventy-two are presented as being well familiar with the post-Alexander Greek world and able to engage it.

These Things Are NOT Like the Other

Yet the *Letter of Aristeas* does not present its Jewish characters as poorly disguised Greeks. On the one hand, it emphasizes how well Greeks and Jews get along. It presents the Greek world as not being threatening toward Jews. It is not to be avoided or derided. It is affirming and welcoming, respectful and worshiping the same God. In it are numerous allies of Jewish people. Likewise, the Jewish world welcomes gentiles. Its tradition is accessible to them. Its God, known by different names, blesses all people.

On the other hand, the *Letter of Aristeas* presents important differences between Jews and gentiles. It upholds Jewish practices that express and maintain Jewish identity in this multicultural yet Greek-dominated world. One set

DOING THE MATH: 72 OR 70?

Aristeas emphasizes that there are seventy-two translators, six from each of the twelve tribes. Yet the translation comes to be known as the Septuagint, which represents (in Latin) the number seventy. How does this happen?

The process is not clear, but there seem to be at least two steps. One step involves a reduction in the number of translators from seventy-two to seventy. This happens in the late first century CE Jewish writer Josephus, who refers to six translators from every tribe (= 72; *Ant.* 12.39, 49, 56) as well as explicitly to seventy translators (*Ant.* 12.57, 86). In the mid-second century CE, Justin Martyr refers to seventy translators (*Dial.* 68, 71) and seems to refer to their translation of the whole Hebrew Scriptures not just the Pentateuch. It is not clear why seventy might be preferred. One suggestion is that the choice of seventy was influenced by the tradition of seventy elders who received the law at Sinai (Exod. 24:9–11) and who God addresses, with Moses, in the wilderness (Num. 11:16–25).

The second step transfers the number seventy from the translators to the translation itself. The earliest evidence is in the fourth century CE, when the church historian Eusebius, writing in Greek, identifies a Greek translation as "of the seventy" to distinguish it from other translations of Aquila, Symmachus, and Theodotion (*Hist. eccl.* 6.16.1, 4). The famous bishop and theologian Augustine of Hippo (d. 430 CE), writing in Latin, says it is traditional to call the translation from Hebrew into Greek the Septuagint, using the Latin term *Septuaginta* (*Civ.* 18.42).

of practices involves eating with gentiles. When the translators eat with the king in Alexandria, they do not abandon their Jewish practices. Instead, the food preparations are made "in accordance with the customs practiced by all [the] visitors from Judea" (*Let. Aris.* 184). King Ptolemy shows that cultural interaction does not remove differences. Rather, he respects them.

Likewise, as the translators went about their translation work, "following the custom of all the Jews, they washed their hands in the sea in the course of their prayers to God . . . as evidence that they had done no evil" (*Let. Aris.* 305–306). Demetrios does not hinder this expression of Jewish identity. He respects it.

When he narrates the arrival of King Ptolemy's delegation in Jerusalem, Aristeas describes the Jerusalem temple, its ritual, priestly activity, and the garments of the chief priest (*Let. Aris.* 83–99). He concludes his overwhelmingly positive—even idealistic—description by emphasizing the temple's uniqueness and superiority: "I emphatically assert that everyone who comes near the spectacle of what I have described will experience astonishment and amazement beyond words" (*Let. Aris.* 99). Aristeas—the gentile!—admires and celebrates Jewish practices.

Eleazar, the Jerusalem high priest, speaks to the gentile delegation at length about the law (*Let. Aris.* 128–171). Although he presents the law as available to anyone, he also upholds the distinction between things considered clean and unclean for eating or touching (*Let. Aris.* 129). He rejects polytheism and the creation of images (idols), explicitly attacking Greek and Egyptian practices (*Let. Aris.* 135–138). The law, he says, surrounds Jewish people "with unbroken palisades and iron walls to prevent our mixing with any other peoples. . . . God hedged us in on all sides with strict observances" (*Let. Aris.* 139–142). This hedging in with these distinctive practices maintains Jewish identity in a multicultural world. It prevents Jewish identity from being swallowed up or overwhelmed by Hellenistic culture.

Yet significantly, Eleazar points out, it does not mean a Jewish retreat from Hellenistic culture. The law itself requires openness to the world. The law requires that Jews "practice justice to all humankind in our acts" (*Let. Aris.* 168). Engaging the Hellenistic world without losing Jewish identity is possible, desirable, and necessary.

These examples hold together disparate elements. There is active observance of distinctive Jewish practices by Jews, along with openness to the wider Hellenistic world and its culture. There are particular Jewish practices that express and maintain Jewish identity, yet Jewish culture and traditions are available to the Hellenistic world. There is differentiation from Hellenistic culture, yet gentiles show respect for Jewish practices and Jews participate in the Hellenistic world.

Translation as Cultural Adaptation and Assertion of Identity

The translation of sacred Hebrew writings into Greek is, then, one means whereby Jewish people mark their identity and make their way in a Greek-dominated world. First, the idea of the translation is sanctioned by Jews in Judea. Eleazar, the chief priest and people's leader, sends the seventy-two translators to Egypt (*Let. Aris.* 32, 46, 51). Translation is a bridge between cultures, an opening to and an entry point for cultural interaction.

Second, the completed translation is approved and celebrated by Jews in Alexandria when it is read to them (*Let. Aris.* 308–310). Translation into Greek signifies belonging to the Hellenistic world as much as it signifies faithful preservation of the tradition itself.

P. Mich. Inv. 5554

Figure 2.2. Parts of Deuteronomy translated from Hebrew into Greek (Wikimedia Commons)

It is interesting to see this balance at work in the LXX. In places the "trans-lation" (plus editing) into Greek removes some embarrassing elements from the Hebrew text. When God sends Moses back to Egypt to persuade Pharaoh to free the people (Exod. 4:18–23), the Hebrew text says, "The LORD met him and tried to kill him" (4:24). Whatever this strange verse means, the LXX Greek translation softens it to make "an angel of the Lord" responsible for the attack. The declaration in the Hebrew version of Exodus 15:3 that "the LORD is a warrior" gets a complete makeover in the Septuagint Greek translation: "The Lord brings wars to naught."

Yet other aspects of distinctive Jewish identity are maintained. Despite a polytheistic context, the translation maintains Israel's assertion of "one God," condemning any recognition of other gods (LXX: Exod. 34:17; Lev. 19:4; Deut. 31:18–20). Yet we find a strangely plural translation of the Hebrew version of Exodus 22:28 into Greek: "Do not revile the gods" (22:27 LXX). The plural form "gods" might be a translation of a plural-looking Hebrew

KICKING IT UP A NOTCH: PHILO'S VERSION

The cultured Alexandrian Jewish writer Philo heightens the element of divine intervention and miracle when he retells Aristeas's story early in the first century CE. He enhances the legend to emphasize God's miraculous intervention in inspiring the translators. Amazingly, the translators, "under inspiration, wrote not each scribe something different, but the same word for word, as though dictated to each by an invisible prompter" (*Mos.* 2.37).[1] So, independently, the seventy translators came up with word-for-word identical translations. It was a miracle! In Philo's understanding, this was the work of "the prompter," surely meaning God, who produced an inspired translation.

[1] *Philo*, trans. F. H. Colson, G. H. Whitaker, et al., 12 vols., Loeb Classical Library (Cambridge: Harvard University Press, 1929–53).

form "Elohim" (*'ĕlōhîm*), perhaps a plural denoting God's majesty, or an expression of tolerance and respect for other gods.

Third, God approves the translation. Yes, that's right! Aristeas comments that the completion of the translation by seventy-two translators in seventy-two days suggested it "was achieved by some deliberate design" (*Let. Aris.* 307). He doesn't quite say, "It's a miracle," but he does suggest divine intervention in its accomplishment. God approves. Consequently, no changes or additions are to be made to the translation; it is the unchangeable word of God (*Let. Aris.* 310–311). God blesses this translation into Greek as showing openness to Hellenistic culture while ensuring that Hellenistic culture does not swamp Jewish identity.

And fourth, the translation is approved by the gentile king Ptolemy. He bows to it just as he did to the Hebrew scrolls, thereby showing them to be on the same level. It is given to him for safekeeping (*Let. Aris.* 317–318). Translation of these sacred writings into Greek signifies that Jews have "arrived" in the gentile world, take cultural pride in that, and are being welcomed with open arms while simultaneously maintaining Jewish differences and distinctive identity.

What was the significance of this translation of Hebrew sacred writings into Greek? For Jewish people living in cities across the ancient world where Hellenistic culture was well established, the translation was a way of making and marking their way in the Greek world. It recognized and legitimated their hybrid existence. They lived with a foot in each of two cultural camps. The translation upheld Jewish identity and practices. But by rendering the writings in Greek, it signified the Jews' presence in and an openness to a context of Greek culture. They did not flee it or fear it at all; yet in embracing it and being embraced by it, they did not completely capitulate to it, nor were they assimilated by it. The translation recognized and shaped a tensive existence, a hybrid life lived in two worlds simultaneously in the interaction of cultural traditions.

The Septuagint and Jesus-Followers

What was the significance of these Greek translations for Jesus-followers? They became the dominant version of the Hebrew Scriptures for the Jesus movement. The movement's respect for these Scriptures in Greek is reflected in statements such as this: "The sacred writings . . . are able to instruct you for salvation through faith in Christ Jesus. All scripture is inspired by God and is useful for teaching, for reproof, for correction, and for training in righteousness" (2 Tim. 3:15–16).

The terms "sacred writings" and "Scriptures" do not refer to New Testament writings: there is no New Testament yet, as we will see in chapters 6 and 7. Rather, these terms refer to the emerging tradition of Jewish sacred writings. The Jesus movement drew predominantly on the Greek forms of this tradition, citing most commonly Psalms, Isaiah, Exodus, and Deuteronomy, though it did not neglect the Hebrew form entirely. Especially important in terms of explicit quotations were Isaiah 6:1 and 53:7; Psalms 110:1 and 2:7; Daniel 12:1; Amos 3:13 and 4:13; and Leviticus 19:18. These references show translation of Hebrew writings well beyond the Pentateuch.

In utilizing the Greek translations, the Jesus movement continued the process of cultural adaptation. Greek was the dominant language of the world in which the Jesus movement came into being, so sacred writings in Greek were appropriate and accessible. This Greek translation provided the movement with theological language, examples, and patterns for speaking about experiencing God in the life, death, resurrection, and return of Jesus.

But in drawing from this Greek translation, the Jesus movement did not passively receive it. In dialogue with it and in relation to their own circumstances, they used it to articulate their own understandings and experience of God in Jesus.[3] In interpreting this tradition in terms of their experience of Jesus, they expressed their own identity and place in their multicultural context in a way that over subsequent centuries would distinguish them from Jewish groups.

3. See also Lee Martin McDonald, *The Origin of the Bible: A Guide for the Perplexed* (London: T&T Clark, 2011), 124–25.

The movement's preference for the Greek translation, rather than the Hebrew form of the tradition, and their adaptation of the translation to their own understandings and experiences, are evident in Matthew 1:23. Matthew 1:18–25 narrates Mary's conception of Jesus and an angel's appearance to Joseph, instructing Joseph to marry the pregnant Mary. In Matthew 1:22–23 the narrator explains that these events "fulfill" the words spoken by Isaiah some seven hundred years previously.[4]

But what exactly did Isaiah say? The Hebrew version of Isaiah 7:14 reads: "Therefore the Lord himself will give you a sign. Look, the young woman is with child and shall bear a son, and shall name him Immanuel" (Isa. 7:14). The Greek translation of the Hebrew text reads rather differently: "Look, the virgin shall conceive and bear a son, and they shall name him Emmanuel, which means, 'God is with us'" (Matt. 1:23).

There are several differences between the Hebrew and Greek versions, but only one major difference concerns us here. The Hebrew version refers to "the young woman." It uses a Hebrew term that identifies her by gender (woman) and age (young). She is a "young woman."

The Greek version refers to her as "the virgin." The Greek term not only identifies her gender but also specifies her lack of sexual experience. Matthew's Gospel chooses to cite the Greek rather than the Hebrew version. This is a deliberate choice because in other instances Matthew sometimes seems to use a Hebrew form of scriptural citations (e.g., 2:15; 12:17–21). Why the Greek version? Because the Greek term—"virgin" rather than "young woman"—has theological importance for Matthew's story about Jesus's origins. It underlines that God brings about Mary's conception of Jesus. The narrative has made this point three times previously. In 1:18 it says Mary was pregnant "before they lived together." The same verse says she was pregnant "from the Holy Spirit." Verse 20 repeats this claim, now announced by an angel to Joseph in a dream. The threefold repetition underscores the importance of God's gracious initiative—as does the use of the Greek form of Isaiah 7:14 in 1:23.

Reading with Jesus-Glasses On

This example highlights another very important way in which the early Jesus movement used the Greek translation. They read it with their Jesus-glasses on. That is, they interpreted the translation in relation to their experience of

---

4. For elaboration, see Warren Carter, "Evoking Isaiah: Why Summon Isaiah in Matthew 1:23 and 4:15–16?," in *Matthew and Empire: Initial Explorations* (Harrisburg, PA: Trinity Press International, 2001), 93–107; earlier in *Journal of Biblical Literature* 119 (2000): 503–20.

the risen Jesus: Jewish Scriptures, Greek language, interpretation through Jesus-glasses.[5]

This interpretation through Jesus-glasses often meant reading passages in ways that would seem to us as reading them out of context. Of course, these early interpreters did not think that. They saw themselves as understanding the text's true meaning. Nevertheless, their approach often produced interpretations that no one else in the ancient world formulated. The key was wearing Jesus-glasses and seeing references to Jesus in Septuagint passages that no one else saw. Just as the translation from Hebrew to Greek adapted Jewish traditions to Greek culture, so the Jesus movement adapted the Greek translation to their own understandings, experiences, and situation. Jewish Scriptures, Greek language, interpretation through Jesus-glasses.[6]

This adapting and interpreting of the Greek translation happens in Matthew 1:23 and its citing of the Greek text of Isaiah 7:14. Isaiah 7–9 was originally not about Jesus and Mary at all. It had a quite different context and referent. Like all prophets, Isaiah addressed his own time. He spoke "the word of the LORD" to a national crisis in his own time, the 730s BCE.

What is the crisis in the daily news in the time of Isaiah 7:14? Judah and its king Ahaz (who dies in 716/715 BCE) are under military threat from the allied powers of Syria and Israel to the north. The very existence of Judah is threatened. What to do?

Speaking on behalf of God, Isaiah the prophet assures Ahaz and the people that this aggression will come to naught (Isa. 7:1–9). To symbolize this assurance, God through Isaiah offers a sign that the "young woman"—perhaps the king's wife, perhaps the prophet's wife—will conceive and bear a son. If Ahaz's wife is in mind, the son is the next king, Hezekiah. If the prophet's wife is in mind, the son points to the future. How is having a baby a sign? The sign shows that there definitely *will* be a next generation. God is guaranteeing the future free of this threat. God promises that the nation will survive. Ahaz must trust God, something he finds hard to do since he prefers to make an alliance with the powerful Assyrians. Isaiah 7–9 spells out some consequence of his lack of trust.

Thus the prophet Isaiah addresses God's good news to real people in the 700s BCE in a real political context of danger and imperial threat. Isaiah does

5. Müller (*The First Bible*, 130–41) rightly emphasizes the eschatological dimension of New Testament interpretation of the Scriptures. Space prevents discussion of this crucial dynamic, which is so clearly interconnected with christocentric readings.

6. Other Jewish groups read the Scriptures in relation to their own circumstances and so produced readings that were not available to other groups. One example concerns those at Qumran who read Habakkuk as narrating their own history.

not speak some words that no one can understand for seven hundred years until Jesus comes along. He addresses his own time with a clearly comprehensible message.

Rather, it is Jesus-followers, reading with their Jesus-glasses on some seven hundred years later, who make a new meaning or interpretation out of Isaiah's words for *their* situation. Reading with their Jesus-glasses on, they see a parallel between the crisis of Ahaz's day and the situation of Jesus-followers late in the first century under Roman rule. The Gospel evokes this past situation—involving King Ahaz, an imperial threat, and the key role of a child in representing God's good future—to interpret the present. Matthew's interpretation announces, "Good news! [He could have said "Gospel!"] God is doing it again. Think about Jesus's birth in terms of that situation with Isaiah and the sign of a child. That birth was God's action in protecting against imperial power and pointing to a good future. Again God is graciously intervening— 'The virgin shall conceive . . .'—and through Jesus will save people from the sinful world under Roman imperial power" (so Matt. 1:21).

Jewish Scriptures, Greek language, interpretation through Jesus-glasses.

Reading a Lament Psalm with Jesus-Glasses On

We see the same sort of adaptation and interpretation of the Greek translation in the account of Jesus's death at the hands of the Roman and Jewish ruling authorities. As Jesus dies, he cries out in the words of Psalm 22:1: "At three o'clock Jesus cried out with a loud voice, 'Eloi, Eloi, lema sabachthani?' which means, 'My God, my God, why have you forsaken me?'" (Mark 15:34).

Here Psalm 22 is evoked in relation to Jesus. Of course the psalm, along with all the other psalms, had functioned for centuries for Jewish worshipers in their relationships with God without any reference to Jesus. Reading with Jesus-glasses on, the Jesus movement interpreted the translated psalm to make sense of what had happened to Jesus.

In the first part of verse 34, Jesus cries out in Aramaic. His cry is then given in Greek, which closely, though not completely, replicates the Greek of Psalm 21:2 (LXX numbering). This is a psalm (Ps. 22 in our contemporary Bibles) of lament, or complaint.[7]

Lament psalms usually feature three characters in three typical roles. The first role belongs to the psalmist, the "I" and "me" of the psalm. This person self-presents as a righteous person who suffers unjustly, lamenting or whining to God about suffering or trouble that the psalmist has not brought on

7. Lament psalms can be either individual (e.g., 13; 22; 69; 88) or communal complaints (44; 60; 79; 94).

himself or herself. The suffering is usually hard to identify precisely but easy to identify with. It often involves illness, personal injury, and/or social conflict for the psalmist.

The second role belongs to God. Initially in lament psalms, God seems to be distant and powerless. Often the psalmist accuses God of doing nothing and not caring: "Why are you so far from helping me, from the words of my groaning?" (Ps. 22:1). Yet the psalmist also recognizes past times when God has been faithful and has actively intervened (22:3–5). But then toward the end of the psalm, a transformation takes place in which God heals or delivers the psalmist. Usually this intervention is assumed rather than described in a lament psalm. The psalmist, now rescued or healed and secure in God's love, expresses trust in God again. In Psalm 22 that change occurs in verse 22.

The third role is that of enemies or hostile people. These people are often unidentified but typically cause the psalmist great misery. In Psalm 22 they publicly mock him (vv. 6–7), theologically taunt him (v. 8), and verbally insult him (vv. 12–14). They threaten his existence (vv. 16–17) and take his clothing (v. 18).

These psalms of lament narrate a typical experience of life and of God. The experience comprises vulnerability, danger, misery, powerlessness, abandonment. Then come divine intervention, deliverance, and restoration. The typical experiences of lament psalms involve personal and social dimensions, as well as relationship with God. Thus the psalm offers a pattern or a paradigm of the experience of bad things happening to a good person. It narrates the suffering and offers the assurance that with God the bad things do not have the final word. This paradigm is known as the lament of the righteous sufferer vindicated by God.[8]

When Mark 15:34 cites Psalm 22:1, it evokes this pattern of the righteous sufferer vindicated by God. It invites readers to understand what is happening to Jesus in his crucifixion in terms of this paradigm involving three actors; terrible suffering; apparent divine indifference, inactivity, powerlessness—but then life-giving divine intervention. Thus it presents Jesus as suffering because of enemies who seek to destroy him with accusations (Mark 15:3), mocking (15:3–4, 16–20, 29–32), taking his clothing (15:24), and putting him to death (15:33–39)—all elements that Psalm 22 mentions. When Jesus uses the words

8. It is used not only in the Psalms but also in Job. Think of the righteous Job, who has done nothing wrong, his three tormenting friends/enemies, Job's complaints and his final vindication by God. A similar pattern of experience appears in Isa. 52–53 where a Suffering Servant, faithful to God, absorbs the suffering from enemies for the sake of others and is vindicated by God.

of Psalm 22 to cry out from the cross about God's forsaking him, God seems indifferent, uncaring, powerless.

Mark 15, though, is followed by chapter 16, with its announcement: "He has been raised; he is not here" (16:6). Suffering is followed by resurrection, passivity by activity, powerlessness by life-giving power. God vindicates the suffering Jesus. Mark employs a pattern borrowed from the Septuagint to make sense of Jesus's death.

Jewish Scriptures, Greek language, interpretation through Jesus-glasses.

Rereading Other Paradigms

The New Testament writers borrow many such paradigms from the Septuagint and, reading with their Jesus-glasses on, reread them or reinterpret them in relation to Jesus. We can briefly note several examples:

- Daniel 7:13–14 presents either a coming heavenly figure or a symbol of God's people, "one like a son of man" (RSV), to whom God will delegate rule over all people. The Gospels of Mark, Matthew, and Luke identify Jesus as this figure (Mark 8:38; 14:62; Matt. 24:30). The identification presents Jesus as the one who will establish God's rule in its fullness.
- Various writings, known as Wisdom texts, envision God's presence and revelation in the world in the form of the activity of a woman, Lady Wisdom (e.g., Prov. 8). John's Gospel especially employs this paradigm in presenting Jesus as the revealer of the power and presence of God.[9]
- Luke's Gospel begins its presentation of Jesus's public ministry by having Jesus read from Isaiah 58:6 and 61:1–2, "The Spirit of the Lord is upon me . . ." (Luke 4:18–19). The Isaiah readings belong to a tradition concerned with Sabbath and Jubilee years (e.g., Lev. 25), which restore human community through release from slavery and debt and the reversal of accumulation of land. The quote presents Jesus's ministry as one of release and societal transformation.
- Moses is a hugely important figure as one who reveals God's purposes in the giving of the law on Mount Sinai/Horeb. The opening chapters of Matthew link Jesus and Moses through the attack of Herod (think Pharaoh), Jesus's journey to Egypt, his testing in the wilderness, and his teaching on a mountain (Matt. 5:1). These and other links present Jesus as a Moses look-alike, who reveals God's purposes.[10]

9. See the excellent discussion of Sharon Ringe, *Wisdom's Friends: Community and Christology in the Fourth Gospel* (Louisville: Westminster John Knox, 1999).

10. Dale Allison, *The New Moses: A Matthean Typology* (Minneapolis: Fortress, 1993).

- Both Luke 7:22 and Matthew 11:5 echo material from Isaiah 26:19 and 35:5–6 to interpret Jesus's miracles. They are not merely acts of power, but also actions that anticipate and enact the abundant fertility and physical wholeness that will accompany the future full establishment of God's life-giving purposes on earth.
- The book of Hebrews especially draws on scriptural traditions concerning the temple, priesthood, and sacrifice in its interpretation of Jesus and of being his followers. It draws extensively from the Septuagint.

Across the New Testament, the writers borrow paradigms from the Septuagint and, with their Jesus-glasses on, reread them in relation to Jesus.

Paul in Romans

Paul uses the Septuagint in similar ways. For example, he heaps up a chain, or catena, of quotes from the Septuagint in Romans 3:10–18 to reinforce his analysis of the human condition as marked by unfaithfulness to God. In Romans 9–11 he employs frequent citations to show that both Jews and gentiles are included in God's plans and to argue that "God has imprisoned all in disobedience so that God may be merciful to all" (11:32).

He also borrows images from the Septuagint to elaborate God's rescue of people from a world of sin and godlessness described in Romans 1:18–3:20. So in Romans 3:24–25, Paul says that "they are now *justified* by his grace as a gift, through the *redemption* that is in Christ Jesus, whom God put forward as a *sacrifice of atonement* by his blood, effective through faith" (emphasis added).

In these rich verses, Paul uses a number of metaphors or pictures to interpret the significance of God's action in Jesus. In quick succession he evokes three different worlds of reference by using words from the Septuagint:

1. *Justified*: As strange as it may seem, this word is a form of the word "righteousness" or "justice" in Greek. At heart, the word is about relationship and being faithful to one's relational commitments. God is "just" or "righteous" when God acts faithfully to God's promises, especially to God's covenant promises to Israel (Ps. 31:1; Isa. 45:21; 46:13). So when God justifies or "righteousnesses" someone (makes someone righteous), God acts faithfully in setting and sustaining a person in faithful relationship with God and with other people.
2. *Redemption*: Like the creator of a fast-moving music video, Paul quickly changes the image of God's activity from one of creating relational

faithfulness to one of God "setting free" or "liberating" those who are imprisoned or enslaved. Again Paul uses a word from the Septuagint. God "sets free" or "redeems" or "ransoms" Israel from slavery in Egypt by making Pharaoh let his people go in the exodus (Deut. 7:8). God changes their state and identity from being enslaved to being free. Paul uses this language to picture God's similar activity for Jesus-believers.

3. *Sacrifice of atonement*: Paul again changes the image. Now he uses a word that occurs largely in the Septuagint in relation to "the mercy seat," the lid of "the ark of the covenant" (Exod. 25:17–25; Lev. 16). This place was particularly associated with the offering of sacrificial blood for the taking away of sin, done on the annual Day of Atonement (Lev. 16:13–16). By using this language, Paul presents Jesus as the "place" where sin is removed.

Paul ends these verses with a reference to "faith" or "faithfulness." In the next chapter, Romans 4, Paul borrows a megastar from the Septuagint, Abraham, as an example of one who was faith-full to God's promises and purposes.

By noting links between Paul's language and only the Septuagint, I am not suggesting that his language and that of other New Testament writers does not also resonate with other religious traditions, political structures, and social experiences. Because of space limits, here I can focus only on his use of the Septuagint to interpret the significance of God's action in Jesus.

Conclusion

Our second date, ca. 250 BCE*, has turned out to be an approximate date, a legendary date, and a process date. Although Aristeas's legend specifies the rule of Ptolemy II (250s BCE) as the time when the Pentateuch was translated from Hebrew into Greek, the reality is that Jewish sacred writings were probably being translated from Hebrew to Greek in a process lasting at least a century or more. This translation process, I have suggested, represented a means of establishing Jewish identity within a multicultural world dominated by Greek language and culture. The translation was both a way of belonging and a way of maintaining distinctive identity.

For the early Jesus movement, the Greek translation that resulted from this process subsequently became a source of theological vocabulary, personal and political examples, social structures, and ideas by which Jesus-followers could express the significance of Jesus. Interpreting their experience by reading the Septuagint while wearing their Jesus-glasses, they "saw" references to

Jesus that no one had seen previously. By "reading" this translation from their particular place and experience of commitment to Jesus, they were able to adapt the Septuagint translation to both inform and express the significance of Jesus and the identity of being his follower.

Jewish Scriptures, Greek translation, interpretation through Jesus-glasses.

The Rededication
of the Jerusalem Temple
(164 BCE)

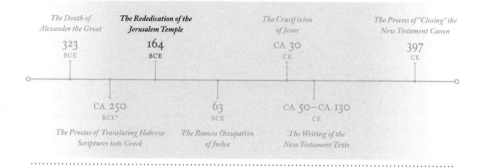

The Death of Alexander the Great	The Rededication of the Jerusalem Temple		The Crucifixion of Jesus	The Process of "Closing" the New Testament Canon
323 BCE	164 BCE		CA. 30 CE	397 CE
	CA. 250 BCE*	63 BCE	CA. 50—CA. 130 CE	
	The Process of Translating Hebrew Scriptures into Greek	The Roman Occupation of Judea	The Writing of the New Testament Texts	

To this very day, Jewish communities celebrate this third key event. The annual festival of Hanukkah marks the rededication of the Jerusalem temple in December 164 BCE. Why did the temple need rededicating? What had happened to pollute it?[1]

We continue to think about the issue of negotiating Greek culture. In the last chapter we saw that translation of Hebrew Scriptures into Greek negotiated Greek culture partly by a combination of using it and preserving Jewish distinctive traditions and practices. Our discussion of that translation process might suggest an easy accommodation to the Greek world. But things are never simple or monolithic. Evident in the crisis surrounding the rededication of

1. Significant for this chapter are the following: Daniel Harrington, *Invitation to the Apocrypha* (Grand Rapids: Eerdmans, 1999); David deSilva, *Introducing the Apocrypha: Message, Context, and Significance* (Grand Rapids: Baker Academic, 2002); George W. E. Nickelsburg, *Ancient Judaism and Christian Origins: Diversity, Continuity, and Transformation* (Minneapolis: Fortress, 2003); Anathea Portier-Young, *Apocalypse against Empire: Theories of Resistance in Early Judaism* (Grand Rapids: Eerdmans, 2011).

the Jerusalem temple in 164 BCE are at least five quite different ways by which Jewish folks negotiated Greek culture. There was no agreement among Jewish folks about what being faithful to God in a multicultural world dominated by Greek culture looked like. Faithfulness was a disputed and multifaceted category.

In this chapter, we begin by outlining what happened in the events leading up to the rededication of 164 BCE: we highlight the numerous and diverse forms of engagement with Greek culture that this crisis exposes. Then in its aftermath we locate the significant Jewish figures Jesus and Paul in the diversity and vibrancy of first-century Judaism. Throughout we engage questions of identity, diverse practices, central convictions, key practices, boundaries, and litmus tests for belonging that were significant for early Judaism.

So what happened in 164 BCE? Why does it matter?

IDENTITY MARKERS

Debates about identity markers and boundaries are present in every religious tradition, including in our own time.

My local newspaper recently featured an article about a group with which a local politician had joined in hosting a prayer breakfast. The group was antigay and declared that "Jews, Muslims, atheists, or any other non-Christian would 'go to hell' unless they accepted Jesus Christ as their Savior."[1] These beliefs function for this group as cultural markers, by which group members distinguish "true believers" from all the rest.

Various groups have taken offense at these statements. Numerous Christian groups would dispute these markers, defining Christian identity quite differently. Plenty of GLBT folks identify themselves as Christian. Paul declares that because of God's faithful purposes, "all Israel will be saved," and it is not at all obvious that in context he limits this to those who believe in Christ (Rom. 11:26). Nor is it clear that God is as committed to assigning people to hell as our politician and his allies. Paul describes God's work in this way: "God has imprisoned all in disobedience so that [God] may be merciful to all" (Rom. 11:32). If "all" actually means "all," declaring who is going to hell may not be on track.

My point is to illustrate that markers of identity and boundaries are part of every religious tradition. They reflect its diversity, and they are always disputed.

[1] "Perry Religious Event Drawing Fire over Host," *Fort Worth Star-Telegram*, Wednesday, June 8, 2011, sec. B1.

Figure 3.1. Image of Antiochus IV Epiphanes on a coin (Classical Numismatic Group, Inc./Wikimedia Commons)

The Villain: Antiochus IV Epiphanes

The villain is the Seleucid ruler Antiochus IV Epiphanes, king of Syria from 175 to 164 BCE. The ghost of Alexander is present again, since the Seleucid line was one of the successors to Alexander's rule. Our source, 1 Maccabees, found in the Apocrypha, begins by placing King Antiochus IV Epiphanes explicitly in the line of Alexander as one of his descendants. First Maccabees does not like Alexander: it presents him as arrogant and overreaching in his power (1:1–7). After his death in 323 BCE, "his officers began to rule" (1:8). This includes the Ptolemies, who ruled Egypt (Ptolemy II Philadelphus was the king in the *Letter of Aristeas*, discussed in the last chapter), and the Seleucids, who ruled Syria. First Maccabees evaluates all these successors to Alexander as continuing his bad influence: "They caused many evils on the earth" (1:9).

That evaluation introduces the chief villain: "From them came forth a sinful root, Antiochus Epiphanes" (1:10). The adjective "sinful" places Antiochus's share of the "many evils" in a theological perspective, identifying them as an offense against God.

So what "sinful" thing did Antiochus do?

Antiochus sought to extend his rule over the lives of people in Jerusalem and Judah. By various means, he set about ending their self-governing way of life centered on the temple and worship of God, and consisting of obedience to the will of God revealed in the teaching of Moses (in the Torah). Antiochus's game was cultural, political, military, and religious imperialism by terror. First Maccabees evaluates as "sinful" his attempt to destroy Jewish identity and community and enforce Hellenistic practices. So what means did he use?

Alliances

After introducing Antiochus so negatively, the narrative of 1 Maccabees recognizes divergent Jewish responses to and evaluations of Antiochus's actions.

Antiochus Epiphanes—Who?

Antiochus surely did not see himself as offensive to his god. Quite the reverse. The word "Epiphanes" in his royal title looks a lot like the word "Epiphany," which denotes both a season in the church year and the experience of a revelation. There was no church yet, not for a couple of hundred years, but Antiochus claimed a revelation—to manifest the purposes of Zeus in his rule. In this case, one person's sin is another person's revelation.

First Maccabees 1:11–15 narrates the actions of "certain renegades," whom the narrator considers to be unfaithful Judeans. These "renegades" form an alliance with Antiochus. They

- agree to adopt Antiochus's legal system (rather than the Torah),
- build a gymnasium in Jerusalem—not for basketball but as a place where Greek culture is learned,
- renounce their identity as God's chosen people, demonstrating this by the reversal of circumcision (No kidding! There was a medical procedure called "epispasm,"[2] surely much worse than having a tattoo removed.),
- abandon the covenant and stop living according to the Mosaic law.

The passage does not elaborate their motivation for this response of making alliance with Antiochus and actively abandoning the distinctive identity and practices of Judaism. But the writer's perspective is very clear. In addition to calling them unfaithful "renegades," 1 Maccabees evaluates their actions as "do[ing] evil" (1:15).

Military Force

Antiochus occupies Jerusalem, "arrogantly" enters the temple, plunders "the golden altar," and removes various temple vessels (1:20–28). Two years later, in 167 BCE, he attacks Jerusalem again, killing many people, destroying houses, taking prisoners, and setting up a citadel next to the temple, where he houses troops and (unfaithful) Judeans loyal to Antiochus (1:29–40).

2. Read all about it in Robert Hall, "Epispasm: Circumcision in Reverse," *Bible Review* 8, no. 4 (August 1992): 52–57. The issue is that male nudity was the norm in both the gymnasium and the baths where learning, business, and exercise were conducted. Greeks and Romans considered the circumcised penis unacceptable, and so a nude, circumcised Jewish male subjected himself to dishonor, ridicule, and social exclusion.

A Decree

He issues a decree seeking to unify his empire as "one people" (1:41–42). Antiochus bans any customs or observances that express the distinctive identity of any people in his empire. For Jewish people, this means the end of obedience to the law of Moses, the collapse of the temple sacrificial system, and a ban on observance of festivals like Passover and Sabbath. They are to "forget the law" (1:49). Instead, he requires new observances involving sacrifices on altars and idols, abolishing the distinction between clean and unclean foods, abolishing Sabbath observance, and forbidding circumcision. Refusal to obey means death (1:41–50).

Antiochus enforces his decree by having inspectors require towns to offer sacrifice (1:51–52). The inspectors place a statue of Zeus ("a desolating sacrilege," 1:54) in the Jerusalem temple and offer sacrifice there. They burn copies of the Law and put to death those possessing it or refusing to obey Antiochus's decree. They put to death mothers and their families who had their sons circumcised, "and they hung the infants from their mothers' necks" (1:51–61). As a result, many complied with Antiochus's edict: they "forsook the law" (1:43, 52). The narrator disapproves. This faithlessness means that many "did evil" (1:52).

The narrative does not indicate why some complied. Did they do so out of fear? Did they do so publicly while remaining faithful privately in their hearts? Did they do so thinking they would gain some advantage through cooperation with their more powerful conquerors? Did they do so thinking that if they can't beat them, they may as well join them, at least for a while until the crisis blows over?

The Hero: Judas Maccabeus and His Family

If there is a villain, there must be a hero. First Maccabees presents Judas Maccabeus of the Maccabean, or Hasmonean, family as the hero. It presents him and his family as God's chosen deliverers or saviors in this time of crisis. Their response is a military option—they fight.

Although some Judeans comply with Antiochus's demands, others refuse to obey. Some of these, identified by the narrator as "Israel" (signaling the narrator's approval), go into hiding (1:52–53). Others remain faithful to their practices openly and defy Antiochus's decree. Antiochus puts those who "[stand] firm" to death (1:62–63). In a fourth response, others like Judas Maccabeus take up arms and violently resist Antiochus's attack on Jewish observances (2:1–48).

First Maccabees identifies, then, four responses: alliances, flight, nonviolent defiance even to death, and fighting.

Of these four responses, 1 Maccabees especially celebrates this response of armed resistance. Its claim is that Antiochus's military, political, and cultural violence is best met with violence. And as the hero, Judas Maccabeus is the great warrior who leads the successful military revolt in freeing Israel and rededicating the temple in 164 BCE. After Judas's death, his family, identified as the Maccabeans or the Hasmoneans, sets up a dynasty that secures and preserves Israel's freedom or political independence for about a hundred years, until Roman control is established in 63 BCE (our next event).

Figure 3.2. Image of Judas Maccabeus (Biblioteka Ro du Jung/Wikimedia Commons)

First Maccabees celebrates the accomplishment of this family as specially chosen by God to secure Israel's faithful identity.

First Maccabees sets out the story of this armed revolt against Antiochus and the securing of Israel's independence. It's a family affair involving Judas's father, brothers, and their children.

Mattathias

The initial violent response comes from Judas's father, Mattathias, in the town of Modein, seventeen miles northwest of Jerusalem. He vows to be faithful to the covenant and the law (2:20–22) in refusing to offer the sacrifice that Antiochus requires. "Burn[ing] with zeal for the law," he kills the king's officer and a Judean who comes forward to sacrifice (2:23–26). Mattathias's zealous action becomes a rallying point, and "many" withdraw to the wilderness. Antiochus's soldiers pursue them and attack them on the Sabbath. But some think it more honorable to refuse to fight on the Sabbath. Unfortunately, such refusal is also more deadly (2:34–38).

But dying on the Sabbath is not Mattathias's strategy. He leads troops in guerrilla actions, killing "sinners . . . and renegades," tearing down altars,

The Rest of the (Controversial) Hasmoneans

The story of the Hasmoneans is a bit like a bad soap opera. Here are the next one hundred years, briefly!

Jonathan

After the rededication of the Jerusalem temple in 164 BCE and Judas's death, the struggle to secure Israel's independence continues, now under the leadership of Judas's brother Jonathan (1 Macc. 9:23–12:53). But military action is no longer the key test of faithfulness. Increasingly political diplomacy comes to the fore as Jonathan works with, exploits, and resists Seleucid interventions, divisions, and intrigues. One expression of this compromising diplomacy is that the son of Antiochus Epiphanes (significantly named Alexander Balas) appoints Jonathan as chief priest of the Jerusalem temple in 152 BCE (10:1–66). Jonathan also maintains power through alliances with Rome and Sparta (12:1–23).

Not everyone seems to be pleased with this appointment of Jonathan as chief priest. A writing among the Dead Sea Scrolls from Qumran (east of Jerusalem) called the *Habakkuk Commentary* (or Habakkuk pesher) refers to a "wicked priest." According to the *Habakkuk Commentary*, this priest's wickedness consists of unfaithfulness to God, greed, failure to function faithfully as a priest, and opposition to the Teacher of Righteousness. Who is this priest? The context and content of the *Habakkuk Commentary* have led many to suggest that it speaks about Jonathan. Others have suggested that it may refer to several Hasmoneans, including Jonathan's brother Simon, as well as Alexander Jannaeus (see below).

Simon

On Jonathan's death (1 Macc. 12:46–53), his brother Simon becomes leader in 142 BCE (13:1–16:24). He is governor and high priest (14:41–42); like Jonathan, he engages in both diplomacy and military action, including victory over the citadel in Jerusalem (13:49–52).

John Hyrcanus

On Simon's death in 134 BCE (1 Macc. 16:11–17), his son John becomes Israel's military, political, and priestly leader until 104 BCE (16:21–24). John Hyrcanus is followed by his son Aristobulus for a year, and by another son named Alexander Jannaeus (showing that the name "Alexander" remains popular in the baby-name books), who adds the title "king" to that of chief priest and rules from 103 to 76 BCE. His wife, Salome Alexandra, follows him (76–67 BCE), with her son Hyrcanus II as chief priest. Increasingly political intrigue and civil war weaken the Hasmonean line, opening the way for Roman rule of Judea in 63 BCE.

circumcising the uncircumcised, and "rescu[ing] the law out of the hands of the Gentiles and kings" (2:42–48).

Judas Maccabeus

After Mattathias dies, one of his sons, the hero Judas Maccabeus, becomes the leader (1 Macc. 3:1–9:22). Maccabeus probably means "the Hammer," a nickname that underscores Judas's identity and ferocious style as a great warrior. Judas the Hammer gains a series of decisive military victories. As a result, he cleans out the pagan presence from the Jerusalem temple and restores it for the worship of God. On December 14 (Chislev 25), 164 BCE, with great celebration, the people "blessed Heaven, who had prospered them" and rededicate the temple (4:36–61; quotation from v. 55).

First Maccabees presents God as approving the sequence of military campaigns led by Judas and granting victory. Violent resistance, not capitulation or hiding or defiant nonviolent resistance to death, secures the victory. Military resistance expresses the desired faithfulness. After the dedication, military actions continue against various Seleucid allies (5:1–9:22). Antiochus dies; his death is presented as punishment for his attacks on Judeans (6:1–17). Then Judas dies in battle, provoking great mourning: "How is the mighty fallen, the savior of Israel!" (9:21).

Differences in Responses

In 1 Maccabees's account we have observed four ways in which Judeans engaged Antiochus's imperial challenge: some actively cooperated, some fled, some defied him nonviolently even to death, some fought with arms. While the last response is 1 Maccabees's preferred form of faithfulness, other writings about the Maccabean struggle define faithfulness in different ways. We will look briefly at two other responses.

Second Maccabees

The book of 2 Maccabees is also found in the Apocrypha. Despite its name, it is not a sequel to 1 Maccabees. Rather, it covers some of the same ground as 1 Maccabees. The key difference is that it offers a very different perspective on how the victory and rededication of the temple in 164 BCE are accomplished.

Like 1 Maccabees, 2 Maccabees describes Antiochus's brutal attack on Jerusalem (5:11–14), plundering of the Jerusalem temple (5:15–27), and banning of Jewish practices and observances (6:1–11; cf. 1 Macc. 1). But then,

Figure 3.3. The martyrdom of Eleazar (Gustave Doré/
Wikimedia Commons)

instead of narrating the military response led by Mattathias and Judas, 2 Maccabees changes the focus: it narrates several stories of martyrs. While 1 Maccabees very briefly mentions some who refused Antiochus's edict and were killed (1:60, 63), it gives little attention to these deaths, focusing instead on the armed response. By contrast, 2 Maccabees focuses on this response of faithfulness to death, or martyrdom.

First, it narrates the death by torture of an elderly scribe, Eleazar. Eleazar resists Antiochus's mandate by refusing to eat "swine's flesh, . . . welcoming death with honor rather than life with pollution" (2 Macc. 6:18–19). Second Maccabees praises him for his faithful courage, his rejection of a path of deception to save himself, and his "good death . . . for the revered and holy laws," which provides a noble example of faithfulness for the whole nation (6:20–31).

Second, after the story of Eleazar the martyr comes another martyr account involving a mother and her seven sons (2 Macc. 7). This poor woman watches as Antiochus tortures her sons to death, one after the other, for refusing to eat "unlawful swine's flesh" (7:1). Their tongues are cut out, they are scalped, their hands and feet are cut off, and they are literally fried to death in a pan because of their faithfulness to God's will. After watching her sons die, the mother is put to death (7:41).

As they die, the brothers and mother engage in verbal skirmishes with Antiochus Epiphanes in which they theologically interpret what is happening. For example, they say:

- To die is better than to disobey God's law and will (2 Macc. 7:2).
- God's compassion is with the ones who suffer (7:6).
- In the resurrection God will faithfully and mercifully raise up the faithful who die this way "to an everlasting renewal of life" (7:9, 14, 23).

- In the resurrection God will restore the mutilated bodies of the faithful who die; resurrection is somatic (7:10–11).
- God will not raise up the wicked like Antiochus (7:14).
- God will punish and torture Antiochus, his allies, and his descendants for fighting against God (7:17, 19, 31–36).
- God will restore the faithful to each other in the resurrection; resurrection is social (7:29).
- The righteous suffer because God is punishing the nation for its sins (7:18, 32), but the deaths of these faithful nine people are an appeal "to God to show mercy soon to our nation, . . . to bring to an end the wrath of the Almighty" (7:37–38). By means of their terrible but faithful deaths, God will be moved to mercy and "will again be reconciled with his own servants" (7:33).

Three things stand out in these theological reflections, which are not found in 1 Maccabees.

First, 2 Maccabees 7 provides one of the first developed statements about resurrection, or the expectation that God will raise some from the dead. Here, resurrection is understood in terms of God's doing justice against imperial injustice and tyranny. Death for faithful people who resist Antiochus does not mean the absence of God's faithfulness. Death does not mean God's failure to act to rescue a faithful person from unjust tyrants like Antiochus. Death does not mean God's powerlessness to overcome such a tyrant. Rather, God is understood to be faithful even beyond death, into the future, in granting new life. Resurrection means participation in a new life marked by justice, by physical (somatic) wholeness, and by social relationships.

Second, this theological reflection sees the deaths of martyrs as having a significant effect on God. Second Maccabees presents these martyrdoms as the key means of moving God to intervene in the crisis brought about by Antiochus's edict. Faithfulness even to death is understood as a way of ending the time of the people's punishment for their own sins and causing God to intervene with life-giving mercy and power to end the tyranny. The martyrs absorb the punishment for sin in their deaths and thereby benefit others by provoking God's merciful intervention.

Third, it is only after these theological declarations about the martyrs that 2 Maccabees narrates Judas Maccabeus's military actions (8:1–10:9). The narrative plays down the military means of victory (contrast 1 Maccabees) and emphasizes that it is the faithfulness to death of these nine martyrs (Eleazar, the mother, and her seven sons) that moves God to intervene mercifully. How is this emphasis made?

First is the sequence in which the events are narrated: Antiochus plunders the temple (5:1–6:17), then come the martyrdoms (6:18–7:42), then Judas's military campaigns (chaps. 8–9), then the rededication of the temple (10:1–9). The martyrdoms provide the interpretive framing for the rededication.

Figure 3.4. Menorah (Tomasz Sienicki/Wikimedia Commons)

Second, God's active involvement in the events is emphasized. Before Judas's army does any fighting, they pray to God (8:2–4). The narrator explains that Judas was successful because "the wrath of the Lord had turned to mercy" (8:5), precisely what chapter 7 has presented the deaths of the martyrs as accomplishing (cf. 7:32–38). Judas declares that their trust is not in arms but "in the Almighty God who is able . . . to strike down" their enemies (8:18). They enter the initial battle with "the watchword, 'The help of God'" (8:23) and "with the Almighty as their ally" (8:24). They attribute their success to God's mercy (8:27–29; as also do the martyrs, 7:37–38) and to "the help of the Lord" (8:35).

Third, the decisive victory leading to rededication of the temple in 164 BCE does not come by military might. God strikes down Antiochus not with Judas's sword but "with a pain in his bowels" (9:5). Without a good supply of antacids, Antiochus suffers much. His suffering makes "the power of God manifest to all" (9:8). Antiochus grants Jerusalem its freedom, promising to restore all he has plundered (9:13–16). After Antiochus's death, Judas "and followers, the Lord leading them on," enter the city, and they cleanse and rededicate the temple (10:1–9). What's missing? There is no final battle in 2 Maccabees in the style of 1 Maccabees 3–4. The sick Antiochus, stricken by God, hands the city back, then dies. For 2 Maccabees, this is God's merciful work that results from the deaths of the nine martyrs. God accomplishes the victory, not Judas's military might.[3]

Daniel: An Eschatological Response

The book of Daniel is also shaped by this crisis of Antiochus Epiphanes's violent imperial expansion. While Daniel's adventures are set in the sixth century BCE, the visions of chapters 7–12 concern Antiochus Epiphanes.

---

3. An expanded retelling of the stories of the deaths of Eleazar, the mother, and her seven sons constitutes 4 Maccabees, also in the Apocrypha.

They offer another response to the crisis, in addition to the four we have already discussed: alliance, flight, nonviolent defiance to death, and fighting. Daniel looks to God alone to intervene in a history-changing way to remove Antiochus's power, restore Israel, renew the earth, and establish all under the merciful and life-giving rule of God.

This is an eschatological response. The word "eschatology" concerns "last things" or "the end of the world." The word "end" is often understood in a temporal sense—the finish or final stage or endgame—and that is appropriate. But the word "end" has another sense: "goal" or purpose; for example, "To what end do we do this?" Eschatology is about the goal or ultimate purpose of God's plans for God's creation. According to the biblical traditions (including Daniel), God's ultimate goal is not to "end" the world in the sense of destroying it. Rather, God's ultimate goal is a world that knows and manifests God's life-giving purposes for all people. That has an element of time to it because this is a future world, but the end or goal concerns a type of world in which God's rule is established. Writings like Daniel reveal such goals in particular crisis situations.[4]

Often in eschatological thinking, writers work with a scheme of several contrasting "ages" or stages of world history. They present the present world, often consisting of several time periods, as not ordered according to God's purposes. It is marked by sin, tyranny, and injustice. By contrast, the final age that follows, the end or goal of God's work, is a world marked by life and justice for all.

So in Daniel 7, Daniel has a vision. In succession, four beasts appear from the sea (Dan. 7:3). Each beast represents a stage of human history in which a particular empire is dominant. The beasts are powerful and predatory. They reflect the author's disapproval of these empires as contrary to God's purposes. The lion with eagle wings represents the empire of Babylon (7:4), the bear look-alike represents the Medes (7:5), the four-headed-four-winged-leopard the Persians (7:6—recall Darius from chap. 1 above, defeated by Alexander). After these three empires comes a fourth, that of Alexander, the Greeks, and his successors like Antiochus IV. This beast is "terrifying and dreadful and exceedingly strong" (7:7). More violent than the others, this fourth beast has ten horns representing Alexander's successors. Then another horn appears "with a mouth speaking arrogantly," depicting Antiochus Epiphanes (7:8, 19–25, esp. v. 24).

---

4. While "eschatology" refers to the "end" or goal of God's purposes, the word "apocalyptic" means a "revealing" of these purposes. The word "apocalyptic" literally refers to taking something out of hiding, thus disclosing or revealing it.

Then Daniel has a vision of a heavenly judgment scene, a council meeting presided over by "the Ancient One," who is God (Dan. 7:9–14). There are two items on the agenda. The first concerns the demise of the beasts. By divine act, the "dominion" or rule of the first three beasts is "taken away," and the noisy, arrogant fourth beast "is put to death and its body destroyed" by fire (7:11–12, 26). God's action alone, issued from the heavenly court, accounts for the end of the beasts' power on earth. God's action ends Antiochus's tyranny. There are no military battles, no martyrdoms, no flights into the wilderness. People have no input or intervention. They wait for God's certain and effective intervention in God's timing.

The second agenda item concerns the establishment of God's rule in place of these empires. Daniel sees a heavenly figure described as "one like a human being" (7:13) or "one like a son of man" (RSV). To this one God gives "dominion and glory and kingship, that all peoples, nations, and languages should serve him. His dominion is an everlasting dominion that shall not pass away, and his kingship is one that shall never be destroyed" (7:14).

After the successive empires of the four beasts, a new age begins, marked by the end of tyranny and imperial rule. In its place, God's rule is established on the earth over all nations through this heavenly agent, who is not identified. He has been interpreted as a sole figure and as representing a people. Just how this happens is not made clear; the heavenly agent is not explicitly located on earth. Verse 27 suggests a crucial but unspecified role for either other heavenly beings and/or for faithful Judeans. However it happens, this new age established by God lasts forever. The establishment of God's purposes is the goal or "end" of God's action.

Summary

So in 164 BCE the temple in Jerusalem was rededicated after it and Jerusalem had been conquered and plundered by the Seleucid king Antiochus Epiphanes. Antiochus had tried to destroy the Judean way of life and impose Hellenistic practices. By now we have observed five ways in which Judeans negotiated this crisis. Some joined Antiochus, others fled, some were nonviolently faithful to death, some fought, some waited for God to act.

How did the temple get liberated and rededicated in 164 BCE? It depends on whom you ask. First Maccabees says it happened because Judas overcame Antiochus by military might. Second Maccabees says it happened because faithful martyrs, those who defied Antiochus even to death, provoked God to intervene. Daniel says it will happen because, independent of any human action, God intervenes, ends human empires, and establishes God's good and just reign.

So What? Judaism and Reading the New Testament

Why is 164 BCE important, and why does it matter for reading the New Testament? We are still a century and a half before Jesus's birth and before he has any followers.

Very clear in the discussion is that politics and religion mix in this biblical world. No one pretends to the contrary. Antiochus Epiphanes's actions were not religious persecutions: he was extending his imperial power. Of course his actions attacked religious practices and sought to impose new observances. But this was necessary because in order to extend his rule over Judea, he had to attack its center of power. That meant Jerusalem, its temple, and its priesthood.

Judea was part theocracy, part hierocracy, with the rule of God understood to be manifested through the Torah (the books of Moses) and the Jerusalem temple and its priesthood. As strange as it may seem to us, the temple was not just a religious institution. It was also the center of political, economic, and cultural power. The Jewish historian Josephus describes its priesthood as the rulers of Judea (*Ant.* 20.251). In all of this, for both Antiochus and Judea, religion and politics are deeply intertwined. They remain so through the time of the New Testament.

So, for example, we noticed that according to Daniel 7, without human help, God ends the rule of the four empires (Babylon, Medes, Persians, Greeks) and then sets up God's own rule through "one like a son of man" (RSV). The Gospels identify Jesus as "the Son of Man," sometimes referring to his ministry (Mark 2:10, 28), sometimes to his death (Mark 8:31), and sometimes to his future return in glory to establish God's purposes (Mark 8:38; 14:62). This last use explicitly evokes Daniel 7's vision. Though Daniel does not make any identification of the "one like a son of man," the Gospels identify Jesus as this figure. For the Gospels, he is the one to whom God gives "dominion and glory and kingship, that all peoples, nations, and languages should serve him" (Dan. 7:14). He is the one to whom God gives "everlasting dominion" (cf. Dan. 7:27) when God has brought down all the empires of the world. Here the Gospels are imitating the same imperial exercise of power that they are opposing. Such a presentation of Jesus in these very political terms of exercising rule over the whole world is certainly not good news for Rome, the dominant empire of his day.

Moreover, in this struggle with Antiochus Epiphanes, we can observe the vibrancy and variety of Judaism and the commitment of Jewish people. Judeans are intensely committed to their identity and practices as God's covenant people. Christians have often not been very charitable or informed about Jewish life around the time of the New Testament. Big misunderstandings abound—such as Judeans working to earn God's favor, or people just going through the motions of mindless ritual in the temple, or Judeans not being able to experience forgiveness before Jesus. You don't die for your way of life or take up arms and fight to preserve your identity if you're just going through the motions!

These passionate acts of commitment are very much tied up with Judean identity. Judeans did not need to earn God's favor—they already had it. As an act of grace, God had chosen Israel as God's covenant people. God's gift of covenant was basic to Jewish identity. The teaching of Torah, including the provision of means of forgiveness, provided practices and identity markers such as circumcision and Sabbath observance along with ways of living that were faithful to this identity. Notice that 1 Maccabees describes those who joined Antiochus as "abandon(ing) the holy covenant" (1:15).

Part of the vibrancy and passion of Judaism in the time of the New Testament concerns debates over expressions of faithfulness. How much contact with gentiles and Hellenistic culture can be sustained without compromising Jewish identity? Did those who supported a gymnasium see themselves as being faithless (as 1 Maccabees insists they were), or did they see themselves as being faithfully open to the world? Did those who remained faithful even to death (the martyrs of 2 Maccabees) think that those who took up arms were being faithless? Did those who waited for God's intervention (as in Dan. 7) think those who took up arms were not trusting God? It's interesting to be aware of the irony that as much as 1 Maccabees fights against Antiochus's hellenizing program, 1 Maccabees as we have it is written in Greek, probably as a translation from Hebrew. That is, matters of establishing and expressing identity in a multicultural world are never easy and always disputed.

And further, it is very clear that Judaism in the time of the New Testament was quite diverse. It was not monolithic.

- Judeans did not respond to Antiochus in the same way: we have seen responses of compromise, flight, fight, death, and waiting for divine intervention.
- Supporters of the Hasmonean line from Judas Maccabeus existed along with opponents. For example, the group living at Qumran protested Simon's receiving the priesthood.
- The emerging canon of Jewish Scriptures does not speak with one voice. Along with the teaching of Moses there are teachings of prophets and wisdom teachers. Wisdom, based often on observations of human life, sits side by side with revealed prophetic and eschatological ways of understanding the world (so Daniel).

- Clearly the temple, with its priestly and sacrificial piety, along with its celebration of important festivals like Passover and Tabernacles, was significant, but not the only expression of the worship of God.
- The New Testament mentions various groups such as the chief priests, Pharisees, Sadducees, scribes, and Herodians.
- High-status Judeans and Galileans, with land, status, and power, were often aligned with imperial power and enjoyed a quality of life vastly different from that of the lives of poor rural peasants or village trades-people and laborers.
- Various miracle workers, popular Moses-like prophets (Josephus, *J.W.* 2.258–263, 286–288; *Ant.* 20.167–171, 188), and rebels or bandits (*J.W.* 2.253) tapped into grassroots discontent. Jesus is crucified with two bandits or rebels (Mark 15:27; Matt. 27:38). A Pharisee named Gamaliel seems to contrast Jesus with two rebel leaders of violent popular groups, Judas and Theudas, in Acts 5:35–39.[5]
- There were popular kingly movements (Josephus, *J.W.* 2.55, 57; *Ant.* 17.273–274, 278–284). Some looked for a messiah; many did not.

All these groups, each with different traditions and emphases and practices, coexisted in Judaism. Given this great vibrancy and diversity, we need to be careful lest we claim that all Judeans thought about or practiced their faith in the same way. Just as there are many strands of tradition and practice across the Christian tradition, so there were in Judaism when Jesus-followers began to emerge as another group. Some scholars have suggested that with all this diversity, it is more accurate to talk about *Judaisms* in the time of the New Testament.

Jesus

Jesus lived and died in Galilee and Judea. How might he fit in this spectrum of diverse traditions and practices? That's a tricky question. Here are four possible answers.

One answer is to locate Jesus in eschatological traditions (like Daniel) and see him as a prophet announcing the approaching end time. In this view, Jesus, like other eschatological prophets, sees the end of the present evil world as imminent, including the destruction of the temple. God will replace the

---

5. Judas the Galilean, according to Josephus (*Ant.* 20.100–102), inspired revolt against Rome when Quirinius was taking a census (ca. 6 CE). Theudas was a sign prophet when Fadus was Roman governor (44–46 CE). He presented himself as Moses and sought to reenact the parting of the sea. Theudas was captured and beheaded in Jerusalem (Josephus, *Ant.* 20.97–99).

temple, restoring all Israel in the coming new age or establishment of God's kingdom.[6]

A second answer sees Jesus as a prophet but in terms that are sociopolitical, not eschatological. Like Israel's prophets (Moses, Elijah), so this analysis goes, Jesus advocates the renewal of society. This view locates Jesus among powerless peasants in Galilee, exploited by landowning elites and the temple leadership. Jesus begins a grassroots village-renewal campaign in which he opposes both hierarchical household (patriarchy) structures and imperial societal structures (dominating power). Jesus advocates forgiveness of debts and return of land; he performs actions such as healing. These renewed social structures enact God's kingdom.[7]

A third answer sees Jesus in relation to Jewish mystic traditions (comprising visions, heavenly journeys, prayer), as a man of the Spirit. Like Jewish wonder-workers Hanina ben Dosa or Honi the Circle-Drawer, Jesus the "Spirit person" regularly encounters God in mystical ways (like the baptism) and expresses these encounters in healings, alternative teachings, and prophetic messages about justice and compassion that challenge societal systems.[8]

A fourth answer sees Jesus as wisdom. Jewish wisdom traditions such as Proverbs 8 identify wisdom as a female figure who comes among humans as God's agent, revealing God's presence, teaching God's ways, and calling humans into relationship with God. Wisdom's work is met with acceptance by some and rejection by others. Jesus is seen as carrying out these roles in his teaching and actions.[9]

Identifying Jesus as "Messiah/Christ" was clearly important for Jesus's early followers, and they read the Scriptures from that vantage point. But what did the term mean? The word "Messiah" is an English form of a Hebrew word. The term "Christ" is the Greek form of the same word. Both terms mean "anointed" or commissioned for a particular role. They do not mean

6. For example, E. P. Sanders, *Jesus and Judaism* (Philadelphia: Fortress, 1985); Dale Allison, *Jesus of Nazareth: Millenarian Prophet* (Minneapolis: Fortress, 1998); Bart Ehrman, *Jesus, Apocalyptic Prophet of the New Millennium* (New York: Oxford University Press, 1999.

7. For example, Richard Horsley, *Jesus and the Powers: Conflict, Covenant, and the Hope of the Poor* (Minneapolis: Fortress, 2011). John Dominic Crossan (*The Historical Jesus: The Life of a Mediterranean Jewish Peasant* [San Francisco: HarperSanFrancisco, 1991]) sees Jesus as a Mediterranean Jewish peasant with a societal vision and program comprising nonviolent and egalitarian transformation of economic, religious, and political structures under the rule of Rome and its Judean-Galilean client rulers.

8. For example, Marcus Borg, *Jesus: A New Vision* (San Francisco: Harper, 1987); idem, *Meeting Jesus Again for the First Time* (San Francisco: Harper, 1994).

9. For example, Elisabeth Schüssler Fiorenza, *Jesus: Miriam's Child, Sophia's Prophet; Critical Issues in Feminist Christology* (New York: Continuum, 1994); Ben Witherington, *Jesus the Sage: The Pilgrimage of Wisdom* (Minneapolis: Fortress, 1994).

"divine." It is important to recognize that there was no universal or ubiquitous expectation of a Messiah among first-century Jews. It is erroneous to claim, for example, that all Jews were waiting for a Messiah who would fight the Romans, causing them not to recognize Jesus. There is no evidence for this claim. The evidence suggests expectations for a Messiah were minority and multiple. While some looked for a Messiah of varying sorts, many did not. Within the diversity of first-century Judaism, we cannot conclude from this important Christian affirmation that all or most Jews shared an expectation of a messiah. They did not.[10] The writings of Jesus-followers supply content for the confession that Jesus is the "Messiah" by spelling out the significance of Jesus in relation to God's purposes.

First-century Judaism clearly embraced diverse understandings and practices. What, if anything, held it all together? Was there an understanding or practice that unified this diversity? Some have pointed to one God, the land, the temple, and the Torah, or teaching of Moses. Another significant suggestion has identified "covenant" as the unifying force.[11]

This suggestion about covenant as the unifying force recognizes God's gracious initiative at the heart of Israel's identity. God graciously chooses Israel for a covenant relationship. God graciously provides guidelines or teaching (Torah) for living faithfully in the covenant. This provision expresses God's commitment to the covenant, to maintain it. Israelites are to respond with obedience. Obedience is met by reward, particularly life in the future new age, while disobedience is met with punishment. The Torah provides for forgiveness by repentance and atonement, thereby maintaining or reestablishing the covenant relationship. Those who are maintained in the covenant by God's mercy, obedience, and atonement belong to the group that will be saved.

In this analysis of the heart of Israel's identity, salvation comes by God's mercy, not by human effort. Obedience to God's teaching is vital, but it maintains its position in the divinely initiated and gifted covenant; it does not earn God's grace. Israelites do not work their way into God's favor by doing the law. Rather, they get into the covenant community because God's grace establishes the covenant with Israel. They stay in by obeying the

10. James H. Charlesworth, ed., *The Old Testament Pseudepigrapha*, 2 vols. (Garden City, NY: Doubleday, 1983–85); W. Green, Jacob Neusner, et al., eds., *Judaisms and Their Messiahs at the Turn of the Christian Era* (Cambridge: Cambridge University Press, 1987); James H. Charlesworth, ed., *The Messiah* (Philadelphia: Fortress, 1992); J. J. Collins, *The Scepter and the Star: The Messiahs of the Dead Sea Scrolls and Other Ancient Literature* (New York: Doubleday, 1995). M. de Jonge, "Messiah," in *Anchor Bible Dictionary*, ed. D. N. Freedman (New York: Doubleday, 1992), 4:777–87, provides a very helpful summary article.
11. See the discussion of "covenantal nomism" in E. P. Sanders, *Paul and Palestinian Judaism* (Philadelphia: Fortress, 1977).

Messiah/Christ

In the Hebrew Bible, *anointing* was a ceremonial way (pouring oil on someone) of recognizing that a person was "set apart" or commissioned to carry out a certain task. So priests (Lev. 4:3, 5, 16), kings in the line of David (Pss. 2:2; 18:50; 89:20, 38, 51), prophets (1 Kings 19:16; Sir. 48:8), and even the (gentile) Persian ruler Cyrus (Isa. 45:1) were anointed or set apart for their respective roles. There is no clear description of "the Messiah" in these writings. Scriptural passages that New Testament writers use in relation to Jesus such as the citing of Isaiah 7:14 in Matthew 1:23 ("A virgin shall conceive . . .") generally do not use the language of "Messiah/Christ" and do not refer to the definitive messianic figure.

In the centuries just before the time of Jesus, some traditions expected God to anoint or commission a special agent (Messiah/Christ) to play some key role in God's purposes. There was no single job description for these figures. These traditions were diverse and relatively sparse. One expectation looked for a Davidic king who would condemn Roman rule (*Pss. Sol.* 17:32; *4 Ezra* 7:26–29; 12:31–34; *2 Bar.* 29–30; 72—identity unsure; probably a king). Another expectation awaited a heavenly judge to condemn the wicked such as unjust landowners and rulers (*1 En.* 46–48), while another looked for a priest from Aaron's line (1QS 9.11; *T. Reu.* 6:8). There were also various popular figures, especially bandits (Josephus, *J.W.* 2.228–229; *Ant.* 20.113–114, 255–256) and self-anointed kingly figures who gathered a band of followers. They usually committed some violence against some elite figures and/or their property, then met with swift and deadly retribution in the form of military attack (e.g., Josephus, mentions Judas in *Ant.* 17.271–272; Athronges in *Ant.* 17.278–284; Menachem in *J.W.* 2.434–444; Simon bar Giora in *J.W.* 4.508–510).

teaching and by atonement. Biblical passages such as Deuteronomy 7:6–16 and a writing in the Apocrypha, the Prayer of Manasseh, clearly express such understandings.

Whether this analysis adequately expresses every crucial aspect of Israel's identity is debatable. And it certainly does not speak for everyone. But it does highlight some very important aspects of Judaism in the first century, the time of the New Testament. First-century Judaism is not based on works whereby people try to earn God's favor, as many Christians have thought. It is not ignorant of grace. It is not dead and obsessed with ritual. Rather, it is rooted in God's gracious initiative expressed in the covenant and the giving of Torah; this requires human obedience in lived faithfulness, in which failure is inevitable but forgiveness is available.

Paul, a First-Century Jewish Person

What, then, is Paul's problem with Judaism? He identifies himself as a faithful Hellenistic Jew, born into the covenant as signified by his circumcision "on the eighth day" (Phil. 3:4–7; Gal. 1:13–14). Before becoming a Jesus-believer, he also describes himself as "zealous for the traditions" and zealous in his initial violent persecution of Jesus-believers. That term "zealous" is the quality that 1 Maccabees associates with Mattathias, who in evoking Phinehas (Num. 25:11–13) violently rejects Antiochus Epiphanes's offensive (1 Macc. 2:23–27, 54). Paul locates himself in the same tradition, which considers violence to defend religious truth as legitimate. But when he becomes a Jesus-believer, he has a real problem with "works of the law" such as circumcision (Gal. 2:15–16).

> Yet we know that a person is justified not by works of the law but through faith in Christ.
>
> Galatians 2:16

> For we hold that a person is justified by faith [or "faithfulness"] apart from works prescribed by the law.
>
> Romans 3:28

For a long time, Christian readers of Paul have thought that Paul sets God's grace over against Jewish attempts to earn God's favor with good works. That is, some people used to think that Paul opposes grace and faith to salvation by works. But this cannot be correct. As we have just seen, Jewish folks did not see themselves as earning salvation. Mattathias and Judas Maccabeus are not earning God's favor in attacking Antiochus. They are expressing faithfulness to their identity as Jewish people in defending their Jewish way of life in covenant relationship with God. Likewise, the nine martyrs of 2 Maccabees are not earning salvation by being faithful to death. They die in faithfulness to God's will, already having God's favor because of God's gracious covenant with Israel.

The key question is this: What does Paul mean by "works of the law"?[12] He is not opposed to doing what God teaches and "requires" (Rom. 2:13–15). Paul tells Jesus-believers to "fulfill" the law, which he understands as loving one's neighbor (13:8–10). He is very proud of his Jewish heritage (9:1–5) and is very confident of God's faithfulness to Israel (3:1–5; 11:25–36). What is his problem?

---

12. For a helpful analysis of this expression of Paul's, see James D. G. Dunn, *The Theology of Paul the Apostle* (Grand Rapids: Eerdmans, 1998), 335–85.

There is some evidence that the term "works of the law" referred to a cluster of identity markers found in the Torah. These markers included circumcision, Sabbath observance, food purity laws, and bans on idolatry. Doing these practices did not earn God's favor. That was already granted when God initiated the covenant. Rather, doing these actions, or "works of the law," expressed Jewish identity and privilege as God's people.

Every people and group have identity markers. Fireworks and picnics on July 4, for example, express identity in the United States of America. Such actions express an identity that already exists: they do not earn citizens' identity. One danger with identity markers comes, though, when they define an identity that does not adequately express a people's traditions and self-understanding. In Paul's view, God has indeed made a covenant with Israel, but that does not mean God cares only about Israel or has withdrawn blessings from all other people. Paul knows this because he has read his Bible. Very important for Paul is God's promise to the gentile Abraham that "in you *all the families of the earth* shall be blessed" (Gen. 12:3, emphasis added).

Some among the Jesus-believers use markers such as circumcision or food-purity practices to define membership in these communities in restrictive ways. In Galatia, some teachers insist on circumcision (taking on Jewish identity) along with faith in Christ. In Romans, there is fighting between some who observe food purity, Sabbaths, and festivals and some who despise such observances (chap. 14). Paul, as a faithful Jewish person, sees these identity markers as expressing only part of the story. He wants to restore a wider and more inclusive identity consistent with an emphasis in the tradition on God's favor to all (Gen. 1; 12:1–3). In Galatians, he argues strongly that circumcision as a marker of ethnic and gender privilege has no place among Jesus-believers. In Romans 14–15 he modifies this position, perhaps because it was not persuasive in Galatia. He does not ban observing Sabbath, festivals, and food-purity laws, but he does argue that neither observance nor nonobservance can be the basis for belonging to the people of God. While some want to restrict who belongs to God's people, Paul sees God as acting for all people in the death and resurrection of Christ. "There is no longer Jew or Greek, . . . slave or free, . . . male and female; for all of you are one in Christ Jesus" (Gal. 3:28).

Yet there is a problem: despite his good intentions, Paul seems to have substituted one set of exclusionary markers for another. Faith in Christ excludes just as do works of the law. But perhaps Paul had something else in mind. The phrase often translated "faith in Christ" can also be translated "the faithfulness of Christ."[13] This alternative—and disputed—translation offers a different perspective. It indicates that believers and their communities are participating in God's purposes when they welcome all people and thus emulate the sort of faithfulness to God's gracious purposes that Jesus exhibited.

Conclusion

Our discussion of the rededication of the temple in 164 BCE has highlighted the vibrancy and diversity of Jewish traditions and practices in the time of the New Testament. Such understandings of first-century Judaism counter inaccurate perceptions of first-century Judaism that have long held sway in Christian communities. We have also seen how both Jesus and Paul belong within the diversities and vibrancy of this Jewish world.

13. Among others, see Luke Timothy Johnson, "Romans 3:21–26 and the Faith of Jesus," *Catholic Biblical Quarterly* 44 (1982): 77–90; Dunn, *Theology*, 379–85, including bibliography.

The Roman Occupation of Judea
(63 BCE)

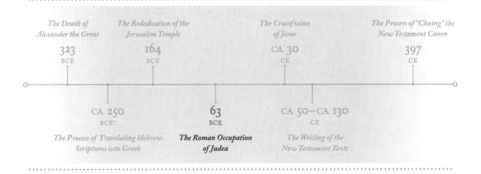

The Death of
Alexander the Great

The Rededication of the
Jerusalem Temple

The Crucifixion
of Jesus

The Process of "Closing" the
New Testament Canon

323
BCE

164
BCE

CA. 30
CE

397
CE

CA. 250
BCE*

63
BCE

CA. 50—CA. 130
CE

The Process of Translating Hebrew
Scriptures into Greek

The Roman Occupation
of Judea

The Writing of the
New Testament Texts

*D*espite their self-delusions of never-ending glory, empires come and go. By the first century BCE a new power has established itself on the world stage. Rome has become the superpower. That doesn't mean the end of all things Greek. Alexander's shadow is much too resilient. But there's no doubt that Rome is the top political, military, and economic power.[1]

In 63 BCE Rome takes control of Judea. In this chapter we look at how this comes about, some of the ways Rome maintains its power, and several ways

---

1. Important for this chapter are Richard Horsley, *Jesus and the Spiral of Violence: Popular Jewish Resistance in Roman Palestine* (San Francisco: Harper & Row, 1987); Lester Grabbe, *The Roman Period*, vol. 2 of *Judaism from Cyrus to Hadrian: Sources, History, Synthesis* (Minneapolis: Fortress, 1992); Amy-Jill Levine, "Visions of Kingdoms: From Pompey to the First Jewish Revolt," in *The Oxford History of the Biblical World*, ed. Michael Coogan (New York: Oxford University Press, 1998), 352–87; John H. Hayes and Sara R. Mandell, *The Jewish People from Alexander to Bar Kochba* (Louisville: Westminster John Knox, 1998); Warren Carter, *The Roman Empire and the New Testament: An Essential Guide* (Nashville: Abingdon, 2006); Richard Horsley, *Revolt of the Scribes: Resistance and Apocalyptic Origins* (Minneapolis: Fortress, 2010).

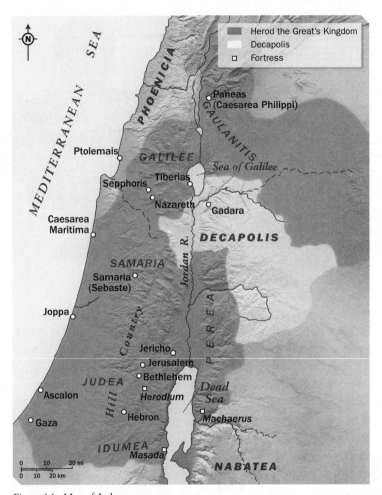

Figure 4.1. Map of Judea

Judeans negotiate it. We also look at diverse ways in which New Testament writers negotiate Roman power.

How Did Rome Take Control in 63 BCE?

A couple of factors account for Rome's taking control of Judea in 63 BCE, about sixty years before Jesus is born.

The first involves the actions of the Roman commander Pompeius, or in English, Pompey the Great. Back in chapter 1 (above), he was one of the guys who wanted to be like Alexander. And like Alexander, he was a macho military

conqueror in the East. He and his armies had
successfully crushed revolts in Spain in the
70s BCE. The Roman Senate then sent him to
the eastern Mediterranean (Alexander's
old stomping ground) to wipe out pi-
rates who interfered with ships carrying grain to Rome, to defeat Roman
enemies in the territories of Pontus
and Armenia, and to bring order
to the whole region. In 64 BCE he
took control of the Seleucids' territory of Syria.

Meantime, to the south in Judea,
Hasmonean rule was falling apart.
When Queen Salome Alexandra died
in 67 BCE, a power struggle and civil
war developed between her two sons,
Aristobulus II and Hyrcanus II. Both

Figure 4.2. Image of Pompey the Great (Jebulon/
Wikimedia Commons)

brothers appealed to Pompey. One of them (Aristobulus) set up camp in Jerusalem. Pompey laid siege to Jerusalem for three months before taking control
of the city and entering the temple for sightseeing in 63 BCE. Josephus reports
that twelve thousand died in the fighting (*J.W.* 1.150).

When imperial power is asserted, there are always winners and losers. With
Roman power asserted in 63 BCE, who won and who lost?

The Losers

THE BIGGEST LOSERS: JUDEANS

With the Roman capture of Jerusalem, a century of Judean independence
came to an end. Almost exactly a hundred years previously, Judas Maccabeus had retaken Jerusalem and the temple from Antiochus Epiphanes and
rededicated it in 164 BCE, as we saw in the last chapter. For a century, Judea
had been independent of foreign control. The Jewish historian Josephus
laments: "For this misfortune which befell Jerusalem Hyrcanus and Aristobulus were responsible because of the dissension. For we lost our freedom
and became subject to the Romans, and the territory which we had gained
by our arms and taken from the Syrians we were compelled to give back to
them" (*Ant.* 14.77).[2]

---

2. *Josephus*, trans. H. St. J. Thackeray et al., 13 vols., Loeb Classical Library (Cambridge:
Harvard University Press, 1926–65).

Particularly, *poor* Judeans were losers. The main faces of Roman rule, at least initially, were the Roman governors of Syria, the client king Herod (d. 4 BCE), and the Rome-appointed governors who had oversight of Judea. Josephus provides an account of their rule in which he emphasizes their greed, exploitation, and enforcement of servitude as recurring experiences for Judeans. Thus, as always happens, the cost of imperial power is paid for by the production and labor of small farmers, craftspeople, and traders.

The Next Biggest Losers: The Hasmoneans

The loss of Judean independence meant the end of Hasmonean rule. Since the struggles of Mattathias and Judas in the 160s BCE against Antiochus Epiphanes, Hasmoneans had ruled throughout the previous century as chief priests and kings. Now they were out of favor with Rome. In the next twenty or so years, both Aristobulus II and his two sons, Alexander (still a popular name after all these years) and Antigonus, made multiple, unsuccessful military efforts to regain their power. With Parthian help, the younger, Antigonus, became king for a short time (40–37 BCE). But then he lost his head, literally, when the Roman Mark Antony executed him in 37 BCE. Even then, the Hasmoneans wouldn't go away—at least willingly—as we will see, but their ruling days were over.

The Winners

Winner No. 1: Romans

How much Pompey the Great cared about a family squabble in Judea is debatable. But he certainly cared about Judea's strategic importance for Roman rule. To the east of Judea were the menacing Parthians. To the southwest was Egypt, a great source of grain. Judea was of geopolitical importance. Rome needed order in and control of this strip of land for troop access, for a frontier buffer, and for ensuring trade across its empire.

In addition, Rome got a nice chunk of change out of subjugating Judea. Josephus reports that Rome required Judea to pay tribute of "more than ten thousand talents" (*Ant.* 14:78).[3]

Winner No. 2: Hyrcanus II

One Hasmonean did somewhat well. While his brother Aristobulus fought to recover his power, Hyrcanus II took advantage of a Roman strategy of exercising its rule in part through alliances with local elites. Hyrcanus managed

3. Ibid. This is a huge amount. One talent was worth about 6,000 denarii with one or two denarii being one day's pay according to Matt. 20:2. Is Josephus giving an actual figure or metaphorically saying "he made us pay, like, a billion bucks"? Note the same amount in Matt. 18:24.

WHO IS JOSEPHUS?

You might have noticed the name Josephus in the last chapter. He will figure in this chapter and the next one quite a bit. Who is this guy?

Josephus was a first-century Jewish historian whose works *Jewish War* and *Jewish Antiquities* provide us with much valuable information about how at least one elite and educated Jewish person understood Jewish history, practices, and contemporary events. He has often been a controversial figure and has been evaluated harshly for his self-serving actions and writings. Yet it cannot be denied that he is a valuable source of information and perspectives.

He was born in about 37 CE. His father was a priest, and his mother was descended from the Hasmoneans (yes, the ones we read about in chap. 3 above). He himself happily tells us he was a bright kid. During the war with Rome in 66–70, he fights against the Romans in Galilee. He is captured after he survives a suicide pact (so he says!). Josephus appears before the Roman commander Vespasian and, ever being an opportunist, prophesies that Vespasian will become emperor. This duly happens in 69 CE. Josephus, the emperor's lucky penny, ends up in Rome with the Flavians (the emperor Vespasian and his sons, the future emperors Titus and Domitian) as his patrons. He writes an account of the Jewish War in the mid-70s CE, in which he presents the Roman Empire as chosen by God. The 66–70 war (which results in the destruction of Jerusalem and the temple) is, according to Josephus, the fault of Jewish rebels and some greedy Roman governors. In this account, he clearly pleases his bosses and blames the rebels, but he is also proud of his Jewish identity. His hybrid location and identity in a multicultural world are clearly evident. In the 90s he writes an account explaining Jewish practices and institutions: *Jewish Antiquities*. People have questioned Josephus's motives, his loyalty to his Roman patrons, and his self-serving and self-justifying accounts. His works combine history with propaganda, self-promotion, and his personal agenda.

to get Pompey to appoint him chief priest, though only with cultic duties. Some fifteen or so years later, around 47 BCE, he seemed to get an upgrade when Julius Caesar made him ethnarch, which gave him some limited political power (Josephus, *Ant.* 14.191).

WINNER NO. 3: KING HEROD

This is Herod of killing-the-baby-boys-in-Bethlehem fame (Matt. 2). He was called, of course, Herod the Great. His father, Antipater, had served one of the Hasmoneans as a governor. Antipater sought to increase his own power by allying with the Romans. By around 48 BCE, Julius Caesar had appointed him "procurator" of Judea. In turn, Antipater appointed his sons, Herod and Phasael, as governors over Galilee and Jerusalem. Power comes from the people you know—that is, through networking, family connections, nepotism; it happens all the time.

Amid continuing power struggles and alliances, the Roman Senate appointed Herod king of Judea in 40 BCE, with the support of Antony and Octavian. He seemed a better bet (more loyal!) than Antigonus from the chaotic Hasmonean family, who had gained Parthian support. By 37 BCE, Herod had, with the assistance of several Roman legions, eliminated Antigonus and established some control. Herod had Rome's favor.

How Did Rome Rule?

Among these winners and losers, we see some common ways in which Rome exercised its power across its empire of some 65 million people. Military power was foundational. Rome lost the odd battle, but it didn't lose the war. Alliances with local elite figures were also foundational, as long as the locals knew who the boss was. Also foundational was the habit of exacting tribute and taxes from subjugated areas. Often these were paid in kind so they were literally a means of transferring resources and goods from a province to the center of the empire, Rome itself. They were a source of wealth for Rome's ruling elite and allies, and a constant reminder that Rome had a claim on the lives and production of local peoples.

The appointment of Herod as client king of Judea was another strategy for exercising Roman control. Herod ruled as a client king from 40/37 BCE until his death in 4 BCE. It was a stormy rule as Herod juggled being a friend of Rome, king of the Judeans, and the destroyer of various plots to overthrow him. One historian astutely comments, "Through a combination of political cunning, good luck, and an occasional murder, King Herod retained his Roman support, his throne, and his life!"[4]

In many ways Herod was a brutal ruler. Does he have any excuses? Let's try a few.

The Romans Made Me Do It

The Romans appointed Herod king in preference to any Hasmonean. The Hasmoneans, though, retained popular support and made continuous efforts

---

4. Levine, "Visions of Kingdoms," 356.

to regain power. Herod lacked popular support. Accordingly, Herod's levels of suspicion and paranoia remained high throughout his whole reign.

He needed the support of the Roman Mark Antony to establish his authority initially, but Antony's wife, Cleopatra, had unsettling designs on Herod's land and rule. Herod had to tactfully fend her off. Then Herod got mixed up in the increasing tensions between Egypt and Rome, Antony and Octavian. In 31 BCE, Herod found himself on the wrong side of the tracks when Antony and Cleopatra were defeated at the battle of Actium by Octavian (later the emperor Augustus). Herod made a very quick and successful shift in his allegiance to Octavian/Augustus, who endorsed his rule and restored his territory. Augustus had Herod's back.

Yet Herod was astute. He realized that with Octavian/Augustus in power, Rome's time to shine had come. He was very oriented to Rome and to pleasing his Roman bosses. He was also keen to help his subjects adapt and be open to the new Roman world.

My Mother-in-Law/My Wife/the Hasmoneans Made Me Do It

Throughout his rule, Herod faced constant opposition from the Hasmoneans. With popular support, they disdained Herod as Rome's puppet. Their repeated plots to regain power clearly fostered his paranoia. But he could not avoid the Hasmoneans. Herod's wife Mariamne—and so, of course, his mother-in-law Alexandra (that name!)—were Hasmoneans.

His very first task after being appointed king by Rome was to remove (assisted by two legions of Roman troops) the out-of-favor Hasmonean Antigonus, who occupied the throne with Parthian support. Antigonus was beheaded, along with forty-five of his high-ranking supporters, who also had their property confiscated. Herod refused to appoint another Hasmonean, Aristobulus III, as chief priest, which greatly provoked Mariamne and Alexandra. Herod had the young man drowned in the swimming pool at his winter palace in Jericho (*Ant.* 15.50–56; *J.W.* 1.437). He put to death another Hasmonean, Joseph, for treason. Herod arrested Alexandra (*Ant.* 15.65–73, 80–87), executed the aged Hyrcanus II for treason (15.161–182), and eventually executed both Mariamne (15.202–239) and Alexandra!

Bolstering his public image as the antifamily king, he executed two of his own sons, whom he had fathered with Mariamne, for treason (*Ant.* 16.66–99). Also for treason, he executed another son, Antipater, whom he had fathered with another wife, Doris (he had 10 wives). No wonder the emperor Augustus, noting Herod's habit of killing sons, is quoted as saying that he would rather be Herod's pig than his son (Macrobius, *Sat.* 2.4.11).[5]

---

5. Augustus assumes that as king of the Jews Herod does not eat pork.

Figure 4.3. Herod rebuilt the Jerusalem temple (Juan R. Cuadra/Wikimedia Commons)

In Matthew 2, Herod is presented as being worried by the birth of Jesus. He wants the "wise men," or "Magi" (NIV), to tell him where Jesus is born so that he can worship him. But an angel reveals to Joseph in a dream that Herod is a liar and really wants to kill Jesus. Joseph, Mary, and Jesus escape to Egypt while Herod kills the baby boys in Bethlehem aged two years and younger. There is no other historical evidence to support any of this narrative. But it certainly rings true to Herod's character—or lack of it.

But I'm Not All Bad

While a client king of the Romans, Herod was also a patron or benefactor for those he ruled. He built many structures in Jerusalem, Samaria, and Caesarea—and beyond in cities like Antioch, Athens, and Sparta, where he hoped to curry favor through alliances. Such projects were good for employment, but they required funding. When rulers build, peasants pay—though he did reduce taxes on occasion.

Herod seems to have been strategically respectful of Jewish religious practices. He set about rebuilding the temple in Jerusalem initially at his own expense, providing employment for many. Despite his own international leanings, he did not try to impose Hellenistic practices. Yet there were areas of dispute because of his need to honor his bosses in Rome. In Samaria, which

JOSEPHUS ON HEROD

The Jewish historian Josephus provides an interesting assessment of Herod (*Ant.* 16.150–159).[1] He begins by reporting that some think Herod had two quite "divergent and warring tendencies within" him. On one hand, he could be very generous and beneficent in paying for buildings and other public works in foreign cities. Josephus has just finished a long section in which he sums up Herod's benefactions to lots of different cities, not just in his own territory but also in Syria and Greece. He continues, "But when, on the other hand, one looks at the punishments and the wrongs which he inflicted upon his subjects and his closest relatives, and when one notes how harsh and inexorable his character was, one is forced to regard him as bestial and lacking all feeling of moderation."

How can one account for these significant differences? Josephus rejects the explanation of two "warring tendencies" in Herod in favor of an explanation in which "these tendencies had the same cause. . . . For Herod loved honors and, being powerfully dominated by this passion, he was led to display generosity whenever there was reason to hope for future remembrance or present reputation." Herod's love for honor meant, argues Josephus, that Herod exploited his people economically because he needed money to pay for his generosity to other peoples, who would honor him in return. His own people resented this exploitation, and for their resentment he punished them further. "In fact, among his own people, if anyone was not deferential to him in speech by confessing himself his slave or was thought to be raising questions about his rule, Herod was unable to control himself and prosecuted his kin and his friends alike, and punished them as severely as enemies. These excesses he committed because of his wish to be uniquely honored."

Josephus suggests that Herod found his need to be honored met more by other peoples than his own. "But, as it happens, the Jewish nation . . . is accustomed to admire righteousness rather than glory. It was therefore not in his good graces, because it found it impossible to flatter the king's ambition with statues or temples or such tokens. And this seems to me to have been the reason for Herod's bad treatment of his own people and his counselors, and of his beneficence toward foreigners and those who were unattached to him."

[1] *Josephus*, trans. H. St. J. Thackeray et al., 13 vols., Loeb Classical Library (Cambridge: Harvard University Press, 1926–65).

he renamed Sebaste in honor of his boss, Augustus, he built a temple to honor Augustus in the imperial cult. On the coast, he developed the impressive harbor city of Caesarea Maritima, with various Roman features, including a temple for the imperial cult. In Jerusalem he built a theater and amphitheater, where he staged Roman-type entertainments (such as fighting wild beasts) and displayed images, contrary to Judean conventions (Josephus, *Ant.* 15.267–276). He placed an eagle, the symbol of Roman power, on a gate of the Jerusalem temple, which offended some. Herod also conflicted with some Pharisees over an oath of allegiance to Caesar and himself that he demanded. He fined them and later put to death some Pharisees who had predicted the imminent end of his rule (*Ant.* 17.41–45).

Negotiating Roman Power: Two Further Approaches

Dreaming of a Messiah

The diversity among Judeans that we observed in chapter 3 in relation to the Maccabean struggle and its aftermath is evident again as Judeans negotiate Roman presence and interference in different ways. Some welcome Pompey while others fight him. Herod gains Rome's favor and protects his own position with both military action and murderous violence against uncooperative family members and opponents. Rome's most prominent opponents are the Hasmoneans, with their efforts to regain power. Both Herod and the Hasmoneans have troops and popular supporters.

Jews negotiate Roman power in other ways as well. A collection of eighteen writings called the *Psalms of Solomon* probably dates from about the beginning of Herod's reign. In them, a section (2:26–30) seems to describe the death of Pompey in 48 BCE. These psalms probably come from Jerusalem, perhaps from a group of scribes.[6]

The fact that these writings are called psalms does not mean they are personal religious writings that have nothing to do with the rest of life. They are very political and international as they engage these contemporary events from the perspective of Israel's covenant identity and relationship with God. Their analysis of Pompey's actions and of the aftermath of those actions is very bleak. The psalm writers are deeply perturbed by the Roman invasion and occupation of Jerusalem and the land in 63 BCE, as well as by the divisions and corruption among the Judean leadership.

6. Helpful discussions include Horsley, *Revolt of the Scribes*, 143–57; Rodney A. Werline, "The *Psalms of Solomon* and the Ideology of Rule," in *Conflicted Boundaries in Wisdom and Apocalypticism*, ed. Benjamin Wright and Lawrence Wills, Symposium Series 35 (Atlanta: Society of Biblical Literature, 2005), 69–88; Kenneth Atkinson, *I Cried to the Lord: A Study of the* Psalms of Solomon's *Historical Background and Social Setting* (Leiden: Brill, 2004).

The *Psalms of Solomon*[7] strongly condemn the Romans under Pompey the Great for desecrating the city and temple in 63 BCE:

> Gentile foreigners went up to your place of sacrifice:
> They arrogantly trampled it with their sandals. . . .
> For the Gentiles insulted Jerusalem, trampling it down.
> *Psalms of Solomon* 2:2, 19a

Though "the [Jerusalem] leaders" welcomed Pompey "with joy" (8:16), the psalmist recoils from Pompey's violent and arrogant ways. The psalmist wrestles with explaining why this dreadful situation came about. Why did God not protect the land, city, and temple? The psalmist's explanation is that God was punishing Israel for numerous sins, including immorality, priests who defiled the temple, and illegitimate kings.

The reference to unrighteous priests is probably a reference to the line of Hasmonean priests deriving from Judas Maccabeus's brother Simon: "They defiled Jerusalem and the things that had been consecrated to the name of God" (*Pss. Sol.* 8:22). Similarly the Hasmoneans are the illegitimate kings, though Herod may also be in view if these psalms were written around the beginning of his reign:

> With pomp they set up a monarchy because of their arrogance;
> they despoiled the throne of David with arrogant shouting.
> *Psalms of Solomon* 17:6

For this psalmist, only the line of David provides legitimate kings. It's no accident or surprise that the collection is called *Psalms of Solomon*, after David's son.

Because of these terrible violations of God's will, so the *Psalms of Solomon* insists, Pompey, "a man alien to our race,"[8] carried out God's purposes of overthrowing their nation and punishing their sinful actions (17:7–10). Pompey certainly did not know he was carrying out God's purposes, and he certainly did not see himself as an agent exacting God's punishment. This is the perspective of these psalms and the group from which they originate.

The psalmist recognizes God as punishing the people through Pompey's actions and their aftermath. But the psalmist remains deeply troubled. Pompey has overstepped the mark in overseeing a situation that the psalmist thinks is

---

7. Citations are from R. B. Wright, trans., "Psalms of Solomon," in *The Old Testament Pseudepigrapha*, ed. J. H. Charlesworth, 2 vols. (New York: Doubleday, 1983–85), 2.639–670.

8. This reference could be to Herod, whose father was Idumaean and forcibly converted to Judaism.

marked by illegitimate rule, greedy and unclean temple leadership, disregard for religious and civil law, and the presence of foreign invaders. All of this has challenged the psalmist's theology. In his world, the righteous are supposed to prosper, the unrighteous are supposed to be punished, the land and the temple are supposed to be safe in God's hands. But this does not seem to be the case anymore. The wicked flourish, the righteous suffer, and temple and land are polluted under foreign control.

Not surprisingly, the psalmist has grave doubts. He wonders if God will be faithful to the covenant God has made with Israel to preserve Israel's existence in the face of such horror. He reminds God:

> You are God and we are the people whom you have loved. . . .
> Do not take away your mercy from us, lest they set upon us.
> For you chose the descendants of Abraham above all the nations.
> *Psalms of Solomon* 9:8–9

So he wants God to act by taking revenge on these sinners. He wants God to "repay the sinner for what he has done to the righteous" (*Pss. Sol.* 2:35). He looks to God to act because there is nothing the psalmist and his allies can do to change the situation. The cry for God's action expresses their powerlessness and alienation, as well as their trust and hope that God will be faithful to the promise to avenge them.

The psalmist, though, recognizes that this justice is delayed. And he does not expect God to act in usual ways in history. Rather, in *Psalms of Solomon* 17 he sees God's deliverance coming in a king. In contrast to the illegitimate Hasmonean (and Herodian?) kings, this will be a legitimate king from the line of David. He is God's anointed one, the Messiah or Christ (17:32). His job description is to "destroy the unrighteous rulers," remove gentiles from Jerusalem, destroy and subdue nations, gather a holy people, distribute land according to tribal divisions, and rule justly and wisely. This is what he is "anointed" to do.

How does he do it? *Psalms of Solomon* 17:24 says he does it "by the word of his mouth." Verse 33 says he does "not rely on horse and rider and bow," and he does not look to "a day of war." That is, he does not wage war to drive the Romans and their allies out and to establish God's rule. But just exactly how "the word of his mouth" accomplishes these purposes is mysterious. Does he shout one day, "Romans, go home!" and they do? Nonviolence, not violence, is his mode of effecting God's will.

Interestingly, this is one of the earliest and fullest references to a Messiah in Jewish writings. It comes out of a situation of powerlessness, in which divine justice seems to be denied. This presentation of the Messiah—and remember that there was no universal or ubiquitous or unified vision of "the Messiah"—does not imagine a superhuman or divine figure. He is a Davidic king; like Pompey, he is powerful. He is an agent of God's justice, who brings about God's rule. The *Psalms of Solomon* endures the shame, suffering, and offense of the present by looking to this final age, with this eschatological confidence (recall Daniel from chap. 3 above). God will be faithful to the covenant. God's justice will be established through this figure.

Popular Actions

Others also opposed Rome's presence. While some were waiting for God to act through the Messiah, others were seeking justice in other ways. They undertook their own actions, sometimes peaceably, sometimes violently, sometimes as a disorganized mob, sometimes by a leader and his band of supporters.

For instance, Herod had placed an eagle, the symbol of Roman power, on a gate of the Jerusalem temple. As Herod was dying, two beloved Judean teachers taught that this image violated the law and was an offense to God (Exod. 20:4). They excited students into tearing down the image. Herod was not amused by this act of protest. He removed the high priest and put some of the leaders to death (Josephus, *Ant.* 17.149–167, 206).

Herod dies in 4 BCE, about the time Jesus is born. Among the numerous physical ailments that afflict Herod, Josephus describes "gangrene of his privy parts that produced worms" (*Ant.* 17.168–169).[9] That sounds very painful. Josephus, no fan of Herod, interprets Herod's sufferings as "God's inflicting just punishment upon him for his lawless deeds."

When Herod dies, considerable unrest marks the succession of power in a tussle between Herod's will, Roman control, and the will of the people. Herod's final will (he had several versions) appointed three of his sons to rule: Archelaus in Judea, Antipas in Galilee, and Philip in territory to the north and west of the Sea of Galilee.[10] Of course his decision is disputed. Antipas in Rome presses the emperor Augustus to displace Archelaus. Another delegation wants no Herodian king, requesting direct rule by Roman governors in Syria.

In Jerusalem, crowds urge Archelaus to lower taxes, release prisoners, remove sales taxes, and appoint a new high priest. Riots break out at Passover, and soldiers kill some three thousand in restoring order. Further conflict and violence occur when the Roman governor of Syria tries to take control of Herod's palace and treasury and his troops are besieged in Jerusalem (*Ant.* 17.200–268). These actions spark revolts throughout Judea. Troops loyal to the dead king

9. *Josephus* (Thackeray).
10. Namely, Gaulanitis, Trachonitis, Batanaea, and Paneas.

Herod attack those loyal to Archelaus. In Sepphoris in Galilee, a sizable band led by a kingly wannabe, Judas, attacks the royal palace, takes its weapons, and loots its property. Judas was the son of a rebel named Hezekiah, who had been put to death by Herod. A former slave of Herod named Simon also has kingly ambitions and a band of followers. They loot and burn several royal palaces before Simon is killed. Athronges also has royal aspirations, a large group of followers, and a war plan. They attack Romans and elite Judeans in guerrilla raids, seizing property and creating terror (*Ant*. 17.269–285). Josephus comments, "And so Judea was filled with brigandage" (*Ant*. 17.285).[11]

Archelaus lasts ten years, until 6 CE. Spurred by complaints about his harsh rule, Augustus exiles him to Gaul. Judea becomes a province of the empire, linked to Syria but ruled directly by Roman governors. The most famous governor as far as early Jesus-believers are concerned is Pontius Pilate, who ruled from 26 to around 36 CE.

This transfer of power in 6 CE after Archelaus was removed provokes more popular unrest. A census is taken in 6–7 CE, supported by the high priest but opposed by a group led by Judas and Saddok, who label it as enforced slavery and argue that their loyalty is to God alone, without Roman masters. The following unrest is severe, marked by rebel raids, attacks on property, assassinations of elite figures, disruption of the food supply resulting in famine, and, of course, vicious retaliation (*Ant*. 18.4–10).

Herod's other sons last longer in their appointments. Antipas rules Galilee to 39 CE. He rebuilds Sepphoris and adds another city on the western shore of the Sea of Galilee, which he calls Tiberias, after Augustus's successor, the emperor Tiberius (14–37 CE). Antipas's rule in Galilee provides a setting for much of Jesus's public activity in the late 20s. He also executes John the Baptist because he fears sedition. The historian Josephus reports that some explained one of Antipas's military defeats as God's punishment of Antipas for executing John (*Ant*. 18.116–119). In 39 CE, Antipas loses a power struggle, and the emperor Gaius Caligula removes him on suspicion of conspiracy. Philip rules until 33/34, when he dies. Among other things, he rebuilt the city of Paneas and renamed it Caesarea Philippi, after both the emperor and himself.

Toward the end of Antipas's rule, an extensive nonviolent protest takes place. In a rare act of aggression toward Jewish worship practices, the emperor Gaius Caligula orders the legate of Syria, Petronius, to install a statue of Gaius in the Jerusalem temple, using force if necessary. Apparently he had learned nothing from Antiochus Epiphanes's attempts some two hundred years earlier in the 160s BCE.

11. *Josephus* (Thackeray).

In response, "many tens of thousands of Jews came to Petronius at Ptolemais" (on the coast of Galilee) and then again at Tiberias (Josephus, *Ant.* 18.263–272).[12] In the context of these large-scale, sit-down protests, they petitioned him not to carry out this order, declaring that they would not go to war against the emperor but that "'we will die sooner than violate our laws.' And falling on their faces and baring their throats, they declared that they were ready to be slain" (*Ant.* 18.271).[13] They maintain this peaceful defiance for forty days while neglecting to plant their fields, thus risking famine and nonpayment of taxes. Finally, at some risk to himself, Petronius agrees to express to the emperor their opposition, and he dismisses the crowd to plant the fields. God rewards their faithfulness by making it rain so the crops will prosper. It is counted as a miracle. Also a miracle is that Petronius's action is honored when the emperor dies and plans for the statue are abandoned (*Ant.* 18.273–309).

Figure 4.4. Head of Gaius Caligula (Sailko/Wikimedia Commons)

Conclusion

When power is asserted, it is inevitably resisted. And at crucial times during the imposition of Roman control after 63 BCE, popular resistance plays an important part in shaping events. These conflicts reflect a complicated collision between Rome's colonizing forces, the ambiguous roles of local leaders, and the rare expressions of the wishes of the powerless people. In play are a host of complicated dynamics:

- expressions of considerable discontent with Herod's rule and hopes for a better future,
- aspirations for Judean independence,
- considerable diversity of perspectives among Judeans,
- Roman insensitivity to local dynamics,

12. Ibid.
13. Ibid.

- local elites trying to please their foreign masters while maintaining their own interests and power,
- the violent assertions of some disgruntled locals,
- and the nonviolent mix of accommodation and protest employed by others.

Jesus-Believers and Roman Power

Through the first century CE and across the Roman Empire, Jesus-believers also face the task of negotiating Roman power. Jesus-believers are committed to one who was crucified by Rome in about 30 CE (which we will explore in the next chapter). So while maintaining their loyalty to Jesus, how did they make their way in this imperial world?

Just as Judeans negotiated Roman power in a variety of ways, so did Jesus-followers. To observe some quite different and complex interactions, we look first at Paul in Romans 13 and then at Revelation 13.

Positive Evaluations

Some New Testament writings position Jesus-believers as quiet, nondisruptive, loyal citizens. As such they are to pray for (but not to) the emperor (1 Tim. 2:1–2; Titus 3:1–2). First Peter instructs believers to "honor the emperor" (1 Pet. 2:13–17) as part of its general instructions for believers to be socially cooperative and to live good lives.[14] Honoring the emperor can involve a number of behaviors such as paying taxes, praying for the emperor, and making offerings to an image of the emperor. Often offerings or sacrifices were offered by the public on significant civic occasions, as well as by various groups such as trade associations.

Is 1 Peter requiring believers to participate in such activity involving idols? That sounds strange, but it may be 1 Peter's strategy. Certainly such an expectation would be consistent with the rest of 1 Peter's insistence that Christians earn a good name with socially cooperative behavior. And 1 Peter exhorts its readers to honor Christ "in your hearts" (3:15), allowing for socially compliant, public actions while maintaining inner integrity. And while 1 Peter condemns excessive behavior involving idols (4:3), it does not condemn idols themselves.

14. Warren Carter, "Going All the Way? Honoring the Emperor and Sacrificing Wives and Slaves in 1 Peter 2:13–3:6," in *A Feminist Companion to the Catholic Epistles and Hebrews*, ed. Amy-Jill Levine (London: T&T Clark, 2004), 14–33.

Paul's instructions in Romans 13:1–7 have long puzzled interpreters. Paul instructs the churches in the empire's capital city to be "subject to the governing authorities" (13:1). He provides a theological reason. Three times in verses 1–2 he declares that Rome's governing authority is "from God," "instituted" and "appointed" by God. Three times in the next four verses he counts Rome's rulers to be "God's servants," who reward good conduct, punish bad conduct, and rule "for your good" (13:3–5). In verses 6–7 he uses paying taxes as the context for his instructions on "subject" behavior.

Paul's emphasis on "being subject" seems clear. But it is not the whole story if we link Romans 13:1–7 with some other contexts. To say that Roman rule is appointed by God is a very flattering presentation of its authority, which was often exercised with terrible consequences for many—as Paul knew. And elsewhere in Romans, Paul is by no means so flattering about the state of the Roman world. He says that everything is contaminated by sin and under God's judgment (1:18–3:20). In 12:1–2, the chapter just previous to 13:1–7, he tells the believers not to conform themselves to this world—that is, the Roman imperial world. And in the verses almost immediately after 13:1–7, he reminds them that the approaching judgment day for the world is near (13:11–12). In 13:1–7 he does not raise the question about how to engage governing authorities that do not carry out God's will, or who do not do justice for everyone's good, but who oppose God's purposes.

These observations suggest that Paul is not offering a universal teaching in these verses, but that he is considering a particular set of circumstances that the churches in Rome are facing concerning the Roman Empire. Perhaps, for example, given the importance of paying taxes in Romans 13:6–7, some are talking about not paying taxes. Paul does not agree with such a course of action but urges their cooperation. If so, 13:1–7 requires compliance in this situation while also being carefully critical of the empire.

Negative Evaluations

Other New Testament writings offer very negative evaluations of Roman power and urge Jesus-believers to negotiate it in quite different ways.

In Revelation 13, the revelation is that the empire is in the control of the devil.[15] Chapter 12 has presented the devil as a dragon who is "the deceiver of the whole world." This dragon/devil attacks those who "keep the commandments of God and hold the testimony of Jesus" (Rev. 12:9, 17). Chapter 13 reveals that the devil has two beasts or agents who do the devil's work on

15. For an accessible discussion of Revelation that highlights what it reveals, see Warren Carter, *What Does Revelation Reveal? Unlocking the Mystery* (Nashville: Abingdon, 2011).

earth. In 13:1–10 the first beast represents the Roman Empire and particularly its emperor, depicted in ways that recall the emperor Nero (54–68 CE).
People worship both the dragon and this beast. Emperor worship was widely
encouraged, but not imposed or mandatory. John's point is that participation
in emperor worship means participation in worship of the devil.

The second beast, described in 13:11–18, encourages people to worship the
first beast and to participate in imperial economic activity (vv. 16–17). This
beast probably represents both imperial and provincial personnel like governors and high-status, very wealthy locals. They were based in cities such as
the seven cities in Revelation 2–3 where the churches addressed by Revelation
are located. These personnel organized and funded various civic occasions,
constructed temples and statues, led processions, were patrons of trade and
craft associations, and served as high priests in promoting imperial worship
and commercial activities. People had to be involved in these civic and economic networks to survive.[16]

The point of this revelation about the "beasts"—the Roman Empire—as
agents of the devil is that Jesus-believers should distance themselves from the
activity of the beasts. The writer depicts the empire as devilish and dangerous. Believers should not participate in honoring the emperor in civic festivals
(contrary to the instruction of 1 Pet. 2:17). They should not participate in
economic activity. The writer is very concerned that the believers in the seven
churches addressed in chapters 2–3 are too snug and comfy in this imperial
world. It's a matter of too much church in the world and too much world in
the church. Unfortunately, though, the writer does not make clear how they
are to survive if they do disengage economically, culturally, socially, and politi-
cally from the empire.

Revelation ends by offering visions or fantasies of the destruction of Rome
and its empire. Thus chapter 18 is a lament that celebrates Rome's demise. It
uses the distressed voices of "the kings of the earth" and "merchants of the
earth" and "shipmasters and seafarers" to underscore Rome's international
connections and everyday economic reach—all destroyed in God's judgment.
Chapters 19–22 offer seven visions or paintings of Rome's downfall and the
establishment of God's rule. One of the pictures is of a final battle in which

16. The second beast's mark (13:16–17) controls buying and selling. It is not a literal mark
like a bar code branded on people. Rather, like the contrasting mark that identifies true believers
(7:3–4), this mark is about loyalty, ownership, and possession. It signifies loyalty to the devil and
the empire. Verse 18 identifies the mark as the number "six hundred sixty-six." In the ancient
world, it was common for letters in an alphabet to have numerical values. The most common
explanation of 666 is that it means the name "Nero Caesar" in its Greek form, Neron Caesar,
but written in Hebrew letters.

the mighty military machine that ensured Roman dominance is defeated (19:17–21). Another depicts the defeat of the devil, the power behind Rome's throne, according to chapter 13 (20:1–3). And another depicts a new city that replaces Rome, the new Jerusalem, which expresses God's purposes, where "death . . . [and] mourning and crying and pain will be no more" (21:1–22:7).

The message is clear: Rome is doomed, and Jesus-believers should have nothing to do with its empire. But while the point is passionately made, Revelation does not offer a program for how to live in a way that is disengaged from the empire.

Revelation is not the only writing in the New Testament that presents the Roman Empire so negatively. The Gospels also have some negative judgments, but they mix those in with some strategies and practices for daily living in an imperial context. They hold opposition and accommodation together in tension.

In the temptation scene in Matthew and Luke (but not in Mark's version), there is an extended dialogue between Jesus and the devil (Matt. 4:1–11; Luke 4:1–11). In the third temptation (second in Luke), the devil offers Jesus "all the kingdoms/empires of the world" if Jesus will "fall down and worship" him (Matt. 4:8–9; Luke 4:5–6). Jesus surely refuses since, as Son or agent of God, Jesus gives his allegiance to God. But it is significant that both Gospels present the devil as having the authority to allocate the world's empires. The devil is the power behind Rome's empire.

Both Gospels engage Rome's empire as the location and subject of Jesus's ministry. Matthew exposes the empire's violence. As we have seen above, one of the ways in which Rome ruled was through local client kings like Herod, king of Judea. Matthew presents Herod's employing spies (the Magi, to find out where he is born; 2:8), lies ("so that I may pay him homage"; 2:8), and murderous violence (against the baby boys of Bethlehem) to remove this threat to his power. Herod's son Antipas similarly eliminates John the Baptist, who has criticized Antipas's marriage (Matt. 14:1–12).

Matthew is similarly very negative about Rome's other allies, the Jerusalem leadership. Christian readers have long thought of chief priests, scribes, Sadducees, and Pharisees as "religious leaders." But such a description falsely separates religion and politics and fails to recognize their much larger societal leadership role. It is precisely this societal leadership role, its abuse of power, and its failed societal vision that Jesus attacks when he says that the people are "harassed and helpless, like sheep without a shepherd" (Matt. 9:36). "Shepherd" was a common metaphor for societal leaders, emperors, and kings. It especially evokes Ezekiel 34's condemnation of Israel's leaders for failing to care and provide for the people.

In Matthew 15, for example, Jesus condemns these leaders for failing to provide for the elderly. In chapter 21:13 he condemns them for running the temple as a "den for bandits" (my trans.), an image that echoes Jeremiah 7 (see v. 11) and its condemnation of the temple leadership for oppressive rule. In Matthew 23 Jesus condemns them for extortion, greed, and hypocrisy. These are Rome's allies, the local faces of the empire, who also represent Israel's traditions and identity.

Not surprisingly, the Gospels present Rome's world as under God's judgment. Drawing on eschatological traditions (like the book of Daniel), the Gospels present Jesus as the Son of Man entrusted with God's rule. He returns to establish that rule in full. In a final battle, Rome's armies are destroyed along with the cosmic deities that sanctioned its power, and God's life-giving rule or kingdom for all people is established (Matt. 24:27–31).[17] Jesus-followers are to pray for this to happen: "Your kingdom/empire come. Your will be done on earth as it is in heaven" (cf. Matt. 6:9–10).

Paul has a similar vision of the certain and inevitable victory of God's rule over any earthly empire like Rome's. In 1 Corinthians 15:23–24, he describes the final establishment of God's purposes in this way: "But each in his own order: Christ the first fruits, then at his [Jesus's] coming those who belong to Christ. Then comes the end, when he hands over the kingdom to God the Father, after he has destroyed every ruler and every authority and power." The dominant "ruler and authority and power" in Paul's world is Rome. His vision imagines the end of Rome's rule. Ironically, this vision of the establishment of God's rule mimics the violence and assertion of overwhelming power typical of the imperial world that is being destroyed.

How, then, are Jesus-followers to engage the empire in the meantime? For Paul, the churches that he addresses in his letters are to live out the good news of God's rule in their interactions with one another. So Paul gets mad with the Corinthians because their celebration of the Lord's Supper reflects conventional, hierarchical, societal meal practices (1 Cor. 11:17–34). These practices reinforce the divisions of power, wealth, and status that divide elites from nonelites in the imperial world. Such divisions are commonly reflected in availability and quality of food. Higher-status people have access to better quality and quantities of food and drink. So when the Corinthian believers gather for the Lord's Supper, they have followed the same conventions with the result that "one goes hungry and another becomes drunk" (1 Cor. 11:21).

17. I elaborate this claim in "Are There Imperial Texts in the Class? Intertextual Eagles and Matthean Eschatology as 'Lights Out' Time for Imperial Rome (Matt. 24:27–31)," *Journal of Biblical Literature* 122 (2003): 467–87.

Paul is furious. Such a practice, he says, shows "contempt for the church of God and humiliate[s] those who have nothing" (1 Cor. 11:22). This practice betrays the grace of God extended to all people equally. It betrays a vision of the church as "one body" comprising "Jews and Greeks, slaves and free" (cf. 1 Cor. 12:13).

The Gospels, similarly, do not call people to abandon the empire. Jesus-believers, for example, pay taxes (Matt. 17:24–27; 22:15–22). Nor do the Gospels call disciples to fight the empire with violence. Jesus prohibits violence: "Do not resist an evildoer violently" (Matt. 5:39 my trans.). Rather, living in the midst of the empire, his followers are to expose its injustices. Jesus instructs subordinates to "turn the other cheek" as a strategy for absorbing imperial violence and exposing its cruelty. Likewise he instructs those who are sued by creditors for their coat or outerwear to strip off their undergarment or cloak and hand that over also as a way of exposing the imperialist and insatiable desire to insult and exploit the powerless. They are also to live out social and microeconomic practices that embody a different way of life by repairing the damage that imperial ways cause: "Give to everyone who begs from you, and do not refuse anyone who wants to borrow from you" (Matt. 5:38–42). Actions such as feeding the hungry, giving drink to the thirsty, welcoming the stranger, clothing the naked, caring for the sick, and visiting the imprisoned are central (Matt. 25:31–46). These are the sorts of things Jesus does and expects his followers to do also. He is "anointed . . . to bring good news to the poor, . . . to proclaim release to the captives and recovery of sight to the blind, to let the oppressed go free, to proclaim the year of the Lord's favor" (Luke 4:18–19). Healing the sick, casting out demons, feeding the hungry, and eating with marginalized folks—actions that Jesus does repeatedly in the Gospels—are not just displays of razzle-dazzle power. They are signs of God's reign or empire reversing the injustices of Rome's world and providing glimpses or anticipations of the sort of world God will establish.

Conclusion

Just as Judeans negotiated Rome's power and presence in quite different ways, so too did Jesus-believers. People often employed multiple strategies at the same time to make their way in Rome's world.

The Crucifixion of Jesus
(ca. 30 CE)

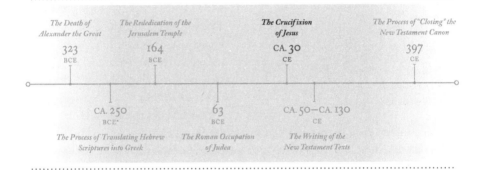

The Death of Alexander the Great	The Rededication of the Jerusalem Temple	**The Crucifixion of Jesus**	The Process of "Closing" the New Testament Canon
323 BCE	164 BCE	CA. 30 CE	397 CE

	CA. 250 BCE*	63 BCE	CA. 50—CA. 130 CE	
	The Process of Translating Hebrew Scriptures into Greek	The Roman Occupation of Judea	The Writing of the New Testament Texts	

*P*eople wear it as jewelry. Businesses use it as part of their logo. It appears on clothing. People sing about it. Churches display it openly. The cross is *the* symbol of the Christian tradition. Do other symbols of execution, of carrying out the death penalty—swords, guillotines, gallows, electric chair, syringes—have such widespread and popular use?

Our fifth key event concerns the crucifixion of Jesus in about 30 CE. The word "about" is important. As surprising as it may seem, we do not know for sure the precise date of this central event in the Christian tradition. We do, though, have a window within which Jesus's crucifixion had to have happened. We know it was when Pilate was Roman governor of Judea, which puts us between 26 and 37 CE. Within that period of time, we cannot be any more precise. So ca. 30 CE is a nice round number. The "ca." in front of the 30 is an abbreviation for the Latin word *circa*, which means "about" or "approximately." So ca. 30 CE signals "about 30 CE."[1]

---

1. Important books for this chapter include Martin Hengel, *Crucifixion* (Philadelphia: Fortress, 1977) (as is appropriate to his subject, Hengel dedicates the book "in memory of

Figure 5.1. Pilate inscription (Marion Doss/Wikimedia Commons)

Jesus's crucifixion has multiple attestations in the New Testament writings and in several extracanonical texts. The four Gospels provide Passion Narratives, accounts of the events leading up to the cross. Significantly, they provide little detail about the actual crucifixion itself. The narratives are quite matter-of-fact and do not dwell on its pain, injuries, or blood: "And they crucified him, and divided his clothes among them" (Mark 15:24). The book of Acts refers to Jesus's crucifixion (Acts 2:23b; 5:30; 10:39), and Paul declares, "We preach Christ crucified" (1 Cor. 1:23 NIV; Gal. 3:13).

Several passages outside the New Testament mention Jesus's crucifixion. In one passage the Jewish historian Josephus says, "Pilate . . . condemned him [Jesus] to be crucified" (*Ant.* 18.63–64);[2] some have wondered whether this text was added or at least edited by a later Christian reader. And the Roman historian Tacitus explains that Christians derive their name from "Christus . . . [who] had undergone the death penalty in the reign of Tiberius, by sentence of the procurator Pontius Pilate" (*Ann.* 15.44).[3]

To understand Jesus's crucifixion, we discuss who got crucified in Roman Judea and why. That leads us to Jesus's crucifixion and the same "who" and

Elisabeth Käsemann," the daughter of Professor and Mrs. Ernst Käsemann, who was tortured and killed in May 1977 in Argentina, where she had been involved in the struggle for human rights); Joseph Fitzmyer, "Crucifixion in Ancient Palestine, Qumran Literature, and the New Testament," *Catholic Biblical Quarterly* 40 (1978): 493–513; Richard Horsley, *Jesus and the Spiral of Violence: Popular Jewish Resistance in Roman Palestine* (San Francisco: Harper & Row, 1987); Richard Horsley and J. S. Hanson, *Bandits, Prophets, and Messiahs: Popular Movements at the Time of Jesus* (San Francisco: Harper & Row, 1988); K. C. Hanson and Douglas E. Oakman, *Palestine in the Time of Jesus: Social Structures and Social Conflicts* (Minneapolis: Fortress, 1998); Bart Ehrman, *Jesus: Apocalyptic Prophet of the New Millennium* (Oxford: Oxford University Press, 1999); David Chapman, *Ancient Jewish and Christian Perceptions of Crucifixion* (Tübingen: Mohr Siebeck, 2008; Grand Rapids: Baker Academic 2010).

2. *Josephus*, trans. H. St. J. Thackeray et al., 13 vols., Loeb Classical Library (Cambridge: Harvard University Press, 1926–65).

3. Tacitus, *The Histories and the Annals*, trans. C. H. Moore and J. Jackson, 4 vols., Loeb Classical Library (Cambridge: Harvard University Press, 1937).

"why" questions. Then we look at some of the various ways New Testament writers interpret the significance of Jesus's crucifixion.

Who Got Crucified?

Crucifixion was, in the words of the Jewish historian Josephus, the "most pitiable of deaths" (*J.W.* 7.202–203).[4] It was usually preceded by torture, often in the form of whipping, and marked by mocking and social shaming. Crucifixion was not for everyone. The Roman justice system linked social status with legal privilege. It understood that the punishment should fit, not so much the crime, but the social status of the criminal.[5] Some forms of the death penalty, such as beheading and even falling on one's sword, were considered more honorable and therefore appropriate for higher-status individuals.

Crucifixion was not normally used for Roman citizens. There were exceptions, such as treason (which showed that an accused person was not worthy of citizenship) or when misused by a corrupt governor (which showed he was not worthy to be a governor)![6] Crucifixion was reserved for lower-ranked, more marginal, and provincial folks like violent criminals and, typically, rebellious slaves.

In addition to punishing violent criminals and slaves, crucifixion was especially used to punish rebellious foreigners. Brigands, violent terrorists, or guerrilla fighters attacked the personnel and property of ruling powers, whether during war or in times of social unrest. Retaliation was always swift and violent: crucifixion was the fate of many.

With the establishment of Roman power in 63 BCE (chap. 4 above) in Judea, crucifixion is one of the ways Rome punishes those who rebel. Rome also uses crucifixion to intimidate everybody else into compliance. The Roman orator Quintilian states that crucifixions are not carried out privately, as is the death penalty in the United States. Rather, crucifixions are carried out publicly, along well-traveled roads, so as to intimidate as many people as possible: "Whenever we crucify criminals, the most frequented roads are chosen where the greatest number of people can look and be seized by this fear. For every punishment has less to do with the offender than with the example" (*Lesser Declamations* 27.4.13).[7] Thus public crucifixion maintained the Pax

---

4. *Josephus* (Thackeray).

5. Cicero argues this point in *Rab. Perd.* 9–17.

6. Cicero accuses the governor of Sicily, Verres, of crucifying a Roman citizen (*Verr.* 2.5.162–163).

7. *Quintilian*, trans. Donald A. Russell and D. R. Shackleton Bailey, 7 vols., Loeb Classical Library (Cambridge: Harvard University Press, 2002–6).

Violent Criminals and Slaves Crucified

Cicero complains that the (corrupt) governor Verres did not crucify slaves suspected of conspiracy to revolt when crucifixion should have been their punishment (Cicero, *Verr.* 2.5.9–13). Tacitus refers to it as "the punishment usually inflicted on slaves" (*Hist.* 4.11).[1] The (of course, male) satirist Juvenal attacks "the ways of women" in *Satire* 6, where he presents a fickle and unreasonable wife who insists on her husband's crucifying a slave even though the slave has not done anything wrong. Her demand for a crucifixion is part of her "lording it over" her husband, one of eight husbands she will have, according to Juvenal (6.219–230). Martial describes a play presented in the newly opened *Colosseum* in Rome (ca. 81 CE). It features the crucifixion of a condemned rebel called Laureolus. A condemned criminal was given the once-in-a-lifetime role of playing Laureolus in the *Colosseum* performance. While he is hanging on a cross, a bear attacks him:

> Laureolus, hanging on no unreal cross, gave up his vitals defenseless to a Caledonian bear. His mangled limbs lived, though the parts dripped gore, and in all his body was nowhere a body's shape.

Martial indicates "Laureolus" is punished for crimes such as attacking his parent's or master's throat with a sword, robbing a temple, or attacking Rome (*Spect.* 7).[2]

[1] Tacitus, *The Histories and the Annals*, trans. C. H. Moore and J. Jackson, 4 vols., Loeb Classical Library (Cambridge: Harvard University Press, 1937).

[2] *Epigrams*, trans. D. R. Shackleton Bailey, 3 vols., Loeb Classical Library (Cambridge: Harvard University Press, 1993).

Romana (Roman peace). This "peace" comprised a stable social, economic, and political order presided over by Rome and reinforced by troops for the benefit of Roman elites and their provincial allies. Sustaining the economic, social, and military needs of this order required the compliance and submission of nonelite provincials.

One of the major threats to this social order in Judea came from rebel groups or brigands. It would be misleading to suggest that all Judea seethed throughout the first century CE with rebellious brigands: it didn't. But certainly Josephus narrates regular outbreaks of "rebel" activity throughout the century by people who thought the Romans should go home. Rome took swift and severe military actions against all these outbreaks that threatened Roman "peace."

Crucifixion was one of the reprisal measures Rome took against rebels:

JEWISH REBELS AND POPULAR KINGS

At the time of King Herod's death in 4 BCE, kingly wannabes like Judas, Simon, and Athronges created, or tapped into, popular unrest by attacking elite property and personnel, and by anointing themselves kings in the hopes of establishing different power structures and access to resources (Josephus, *Ant.* 17.269–285).

Midway through the first century CE, when Felix was governor (52–60 CE), Josephus reports widespread outbreaks of protest. These protests took various forms. Not every Judean took up arms by any means. Studies show that commonly peasants do not resort to violence because they know it will not succeed. They find nonviolent and disguised means of protest, like spreading rumors, evading taxes, feigning compliance, and creating fantasies of revenge and justice. Uncommon outbreaks of violence suggest harsh circumstances and desperation for some.

Among those whom Josephus mentions are the Sicarii, who carried short daggers under their cloaks and mingled with crowds to get close to important figures, whom they assassinated. One of their victims was the chief priest, Jonathan. Others, whom Josephus calls false prophets (thereby showing his disdain for them), claimed divine inspiration in seeking deliverance from Roman rule. Others attacked Jerusalem directly (*J.W.* 2.254–263). Rome repelled all of these. Then,

> No sooner were these disorders reduced than the inflammation ... broke out again in another quarter. The imposters and brigands, banding together, incited numbers to revolt, exhorting them to assert their independence, and threatening to kill any who submitted to Roman domination and forcibly to suppress those who voluntarily accepted servitude.
>
> Distributing themselves in companies throughout the country, they looted the houses of the wealthy, murdered their owners, and set the villages on fire.
>
> *Jewish War* 2. 264–265[1]

Widespread war against Rome breaks out in the next decade, in 66–70 CE. Several Judean leaders and factions emerge amid much internal infighting. After a lengthy siege of Jerusalem in 69–70, Rome crushes the rebels, destroys Jerusalem, and burns the temple, whose rebuilding, started by King Herod, has only just been completed.

[1] *Josephus*, trans. H. St. J. Thackeray et al., 13 vols., Loeb Classical Library (Cambridge: Harvard University Press, 1926–65).

- After the death of Herod in 4 BCE, several figures declare themselves kings, rally supporters, attack property and people, and challenge Roman rule. Varus, the governor or legate of Syria, imprisons some supporters but crucifies the most threatening, some two thousand insurrectionists, according to Josephus (*Ant.* 17.285, 295; *J.W.* 2.75).

- A Roman governor, Tiberius Alexander (that name again!), who exercises power in 46–48 CE, crucifies James and Simon, the sons of Judas the Galilean. Josephus reminds his readers that Judas had led a revolt against the imposition of Roman "slavery" after Herod's son Archelaus was removed from ruling Judea in 6 CE, while the census was being taken (*Ant.* 18.4–10; 20.102). Josephus, unfortunately, forgets to tell us why James and Simon were put on trial and then crucified. The best guess is that they followed in their father's footsteps.

- Quadratus, the governor of Syria when Cumanus was governor of Judea (49–52?), crucifies both Samaritans and Judeans who have "taken part in [a] rebellion" (*Ant.* 20.129; *J.W.* 2.241–244).[8]

- During the decade of the 50s, Governor Felix encounters growing numbers of rebels. "Of the brigands whom he crucified, and of the common people who were convicted of complicity with them and punished by him, the number was incalculable" (*J.W.* 2.253).[9] There were so many rebels that every day Felix "put to death many of these imposters and brigands" (*Ant.* 20.160–161).[10]

- Governor Florus (64–66 CE) continues to fan unrest, with the result that war breaks out in 66 CE. He raids the Jerusalem temple treasury. Tensions increase, and he sends soldiers to attack the upper market in Jerusalem. "Many of the peaceable citizens were arrested and brought before Florus, who had them first scourged and then crucified." Things get worse in Josephus's elite perspective when Florus whips and "nails to the cross men of equestrian rank, men who, if Jews by birth, were at least invested with that Roman dignity" (*J.W.* 2.306–308).[11] Why is Josephus so offended of men of equestrian rank? Because he knows crucifixion is for nonelites, not for men of this elevated rank. This mode of execution adds insult and shame to fatal injury. But why would Governor Florus do such a thing? Perhaps because he was incompetent, insensitive, and (to use Josephus's word) cruel. Or perhaps because he regarded their actions as treasonous in challenging Roman power, and so their crucifixion was justified in his eyes.

- During the war (66–70 CE), the Roman general Vespasian, soon to be emperor in 69 CE, crucifies a "smiling" Jewish soldier/rebel who refuses to give up any information (*J.W.* 3.320–321).

8. *Josephus* (Thackeray).
9. Ibid.
10. Ibid.
11. Ibid.

How Did Crucified People Die?

There does not seem to have been a set procedure for crucifixion. Often victims were whipped and then publicly paraded to the place of crucifixion. They seem to have been crucified in different positions. Josephus asserts that Roman soldiers "amused themselves" by crucifying victims in various positions (Josephus, *J. W.* 5.451).[1] There have been debates about whether nails through the human palm could hold a victim in place without excessive tearing of the flesh, whether victims were nailed through the wrist and/or tied with ropes, whether legs were extended or bent.

The cause of death has also been debated. An older theory claimed that victims died of asphyxiation or suffocation. The extended arms impacted the chest and made breathing out impossible. The person died quickly. More contemporary approaches favor the explanation that a victim died of shock. First was the mental agony of anticipating crucifixion. Then there was the whipping, which traumatized nerves, skin, and muscles, causing sweating, seizures, loss of fluid, and exhaustion. The stumbling walk to the crucifixion site and having hands and feet nailed to the cross exacerbated these symptoms.[2]

[1] *Josephus*, trans. H. St. J. Thackeray et al., 13 vols., Loeb Classical Library (Cambridge: Harvard University Press, 1926–65).

[2] For discussion and details, see Vassilios Tzaferis, "Crucifixion—The Archaeological Evidence," *Biblical Archaeological Review* 11 (1985): 44–53; Frederick Zugibe, "Two Questions about Crucifixion: Does the Victim Die of Asphyxiation? Would Nails in the Hand Hold the Weight of the Body?" *Bible Review* 5 (1989): 34–43. On burial for crucifixion victims, see John Granger Cook, "Crucifixion and Burial," *New Testament Studies* 57 (2011): 193–213.

- During the war, various Roman commanders, including Vespasian's son Titus, use crucifixion to intimidate Judeans. Titus crucifies "five hundred or sometimes more" daily outside Jerusalem during the siege of 69–70 to induce Jerusalem to surrender (*J. W.* 5.289, 449–451).[12]
- With all these crucifixions—and, of course, the surviving record is only ever partial—it is surprising that archaeologists have found almost no skeletons of crucified people. There is, though, at least one such skeleton, discovered in 1968 to the northeast of Jerusalem. The skeleton is of a twenty-four to twenty-eight-year-old man named Jehohanan, who was about five feet six inches tall. Jehohanan's leg bones were broken, and both heel bones had an iron nail driven through them. Attached to the heel bone is a fragment of olive wood. He was crucified sometime in

12. Ibid.

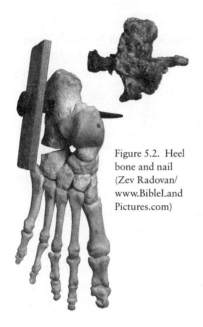

Figure 5.2. Heel bone and nail (Zev Radovan/ www.BibleLand Pictures.com)

the first century CE, either during one of the large-scale crucifixions of rebels mentioned above, or in a small-scale crucifixion for a similar offense.

Who got crucified? People of low status, slaves, violent criminals, and rebels who threatened and opposed Rome's rule. Crucifixion was the ultimate way of saying to someone: "We don't want you in our midst." It's not surprising that books on crucifixion are shelved in the library with other books having titles such as *A History of Capital Punishment*, *A History of the Guillotine*, *The Hanged Man*, and *A History of Torture and Execution*. This is the context, then, in which to understand Jesus's crucifixion.

Jesus's Crucifixion ca. 30 CE: Why?

In addition to the mode of his death (crucifixion), several other observations indicate that Jesus was crucified as a rebel opposed to Rome's rule.

One observation concerns those with whom Jesus is crucified. In both Mark (15:27) and Matthew (27:38), Jesus is crucified with two "bandits," or rebels. Luke identifies them with a more general word that means "criminals" or "evildoers" (23:32–33, 39), while John is much more vague in identifying them as "two others" (19:18, 32). The word that Matthew and Mark use, translated as "bandits," is the same term that Josephus uses to identify the rebels or violent terrorists or guerrilla freedom fighters that have featured in the discussion above. As we have seen, these figures who rebel against Roman rule invariably end up dead either as a result of attacks from Roman or local troops or by crucifixion. Jesus is crucified with two such people. Who you are is told by the company you keep.

A second observation clarifies why Jesus was crucified as a rebel. All of the Gospel accounts record Pilate as placing a notice on the cross identifying Jesus as "King of the Judeans" (my trans.). Matthew 27:37 reads, "Over his head they put the charge against him, which read, 'This is Jesus, the King of the Judeans'" (my trans.). Mark (15:26) and Luke (23:38) say the same thing.

John draws attention to this charge: "Pilate also had an inscription written and put on the cross. It read, 'Jesus of Nazareth, the King of the Judeans'" (John 19:19 my trans.). John then reports that it was written in three languages so everyone could read it (19:20). The chief priests want it rewritten to clarify that Jesus *claimed* to be king of the Judeans rather than declaring that he actually *was* king (19:21). Pilate refuses their request (19:22).

This charge of being "King of the Judeans," displayed on the cross, has featured in the confrontation between Jesus and Pilate that leads up to the cross. In all four versions, Pilate asks Jesus directly about being "King of the Judeans" (my trans.; Matt. 27:11; Mark 15:2; Luke 23:3; John 18:33). Soldiers mock Jesus as "King of the Judeans" (my trans.; Matt. 27:29–31; Mark 15:16–20; Luke 23:36–37; John 19:2–3). Matthew's account of Jesus's crucifixion repeats the term three times, Mark's five times, Luke's three times, and John's seven times. Such repetition clearly indicates that it is an important term. But why would being identified as "King of the Judeans" get him mocked and crucified?

First, it's a matter of endorsement or authorization. If Rome wants a client king to rule over a part of its empire, it appoints that king. There is no other way to be king in Rome's empire. Without Rome's blessing, there is no kingship. In the last chapter, we saw that in 40 BCE Rome appointed Herod to be its client king. When Herod died in 4 BCE, Rome approved Herod's son Archelaus to rule Judea. When that didn't work out, Rome removed Archelaus in 6 CE. We also saw that at Herod's death, kingly wannabes like Judas, Simon, and Athronges emerged without Rome's sanction. They were hunted down and killed.

When full-scale war with Rome broke out in 66–70, kingly figures appeared and were treated the same way. The leading kingly figure was Simon bar Giora, whose followers obeyed "his command as to a king" (*J.W.* 4.510).[13] Dressed as a king, Simon eventually surrendered to the Romans (*J.W.* 7.29). They executed him as an illegitimate and rebel king of the defeated people (*J.W.* 7.154). Simon had made himself king without Rome's sanction. Rome regarded it as an act of rebellion and threat to Roman power. Simon was executed.

Second, Jesus's crucifixion as "King of the Judeans" indicates that he was understood to have exercised leadership and rule that breached Rome's authority. He was understood to have claimed kingship without Rome's say-so. No empire tolerates those who claim unsanctioned rule. Lacking Rome's endorsement, Jesus the rebel was crucified.

Third, there is the role of Barabbas. Pilate offers to release either Jesus or "a notorious prisoner," Barabbas (Matt. 27:15–26; Mark 15:6–15; Luke

13. Ibid.

Figure 5.3. Image of crucifixion (Rafael
Pi Belda/Wikimedia Commons)

23:18–25). Mark says that Barabbas "was
in prison with the rebels who had committed murder during the insurrection" (Mark
15:7; largely repeated in Luke 23:19). John
explicitly identifies Barabbas as "a bandit,"
or rebel (John 18:40). Jesus and Barabbas
are, in Pilate's view, a fair exchange. Like
for like.

Jesus the Rebel King

This is not a common Sunday school image
of Jesus. It's certainly not "Gentle Jesus,
meek and mild." But people didn't get crucified for being gentle or spiritual or for saying
their prayers. They got crucified for being
understood to be rebels. What did Jesus do
in his public activity to be crucified as a rebel king? The question is worth
pursuing because, according to the Gospels, Jesus did not aggressively and
publicly proclaim himself as "King of the Judeans" (my trans.).[14] Without
trying to cover everything, I'll mention three factors.

Proclaiming the Kingdom/Empire of God

The kingdom of God was the theme song of Jesus's public activity. At the
beginning of his ministry, he announced, referring to himself and his public
activity, that "the kingdom of God has come near" (Mark 1:15). He talked
about the kingdom of God, or God's rule, in parables (Mark 4). He dem-
onstrated it in healing people, feeding people, casting out demons, and welcoming marginalized and excluded outsiders to meals. He taught his followers
to pray to God, "Your kingdom come" (Matt. 6:10; Luke 11:2). His language
evoked a long tradition of God as king of all the nations and especially of
the nation of Israel. It evoked a tradition of Israel's kings, who were anointed
or commissioned ("messiahed") to represent God's rule among the people.

Why would such good and life-changing teaching and actions get him crucified? The answer is clear: because ruling powers get very nervous when someone
starts advocating another kingdom or empire. Kingdoms require kings.

14. The phrase appears in the Gospels only in the Passion Narratives and in Matt. 2:2, where
the "wise men" use it.

The language of "kingdom" sounds quaint and harmless to us. Contemporary interpreters of the New Testament usually spiritualize, individualize, and interiorize Jesus's talk of "the kingdom" to mean "Jesus rules in my heart" or "Jesus is the king of my life." But the language that Jesus is using is much more wide-ranging than that. The noun that we translate as "kingdom" is commonly translated in the biblical tradition as "empire." It refers to empires like that of Babylon, the Medes, Persia, and Greece (Dan. 2:37–45), Alexander the Great (1 Macc. 1:1–6), Antiochus Epiphanes (1 Macc. 1:16), and Rome (Josephus, *J.W.* 5.409). That context gives Jesus's use of the word a very different meaning.

When Jesus speaks of the "empire of God," he does so in the context of the empire of Rome, which rules the Mediterranean world. The language of empire suggests that God's rule is not only personal and interior but also involves the nations, who are accountable to God (Matt. 25:31–46; note v. 32, "the nations"). It has political, social, economic, and cultural dimensions. If you were an official like a governor or military commander who got out of bed every day knowing you were the face of the Roman Empire in the province of Judea, you would become very sensitive to anyone talking about or identifying with another empire.

Rome's Jerusalem Allies

As we have explained, Rome liked to rule by making alliances with local elites. Rome shared its power and benefits as long as everyone knew who was boss. In Judea, this strategy meant alliances with the Jerusalem-based priestly establishment, whom Josephus describes as the leaders of Judea (*Ant.* 20.251). The Roman governors appointed the chief priests and stored the priestly garments in the fortress next to the temple. The chief priest had to go next door to get dressed. This ensured supervision and a constant reminder of who was the boss. Caiaphas remained chief priest from 18 to 36 CE—which might tell you something about his prayer life but certainly tells you he had great political smarts in pleasing his Roman bosses. Yet, fundamentally, both the Roman governors and the chief priests groups were good allies because both wanted to maintain their power and interests by defending the current societal structure.

Throughout the Gospel accounts, Jesus conflicts with the Jerusalem leadership group and their agents. Central to the conflicts are competing interpretations of God's purposes and societal practices. For example, in Matthew 15:5–6 Jesus criticizes the leaders' practice of blessing resources that were taken away from elderly and needy parents and given to God (and the temple and priests).

The most significant conflict comes after Jesus enters Jerusalem on Palm Sunday and goes to the temple, the basis of their power (Matt. 21:12–17). He overturns the tables of the money changers and then quotes from Isaiah 56:7 and Jeremiah 7:11 in condemning the temple as a "den for bandits/ robbers." He attacks the leaders as those who exploit the people. By citing Jeremiah 7—a sustained prophetic attack on the temple leadership for oppressing the poor and seeking protection in the temple—he presents the leaders as condemned by God. This is not the way to make friends and network effectively.

Furthermore, just a couple of chapters later, he announces that the temple will be destroyed (Matt. 24:1–4). The basis of the Jerusalem leaders' power will disappear. His declaration effectively announces God's imminent judgment on the temple. Such declarations will get the declarer killed.

These leaders, allies of Rome, cannot tolerate such an attack. Jesus opposes and alienates the powerful, Rome-allied temple leadership. His crucifixion is inevitable.

The interesting thing to observe is how the Jerusalem leaders and the Roman governor work together as allies to bring about Jesus's crucifixion. The tension mounts as Jesus tells parables against the leaders (Matt. 21–22), curses their hypocrisy (chap. 23), and announces the end of their world (chaps. 24–25). The leaders hand Jesus over to Pilate for execution since the governor retains the right to execute (John 18:31).

This interaction between Roman governor and Jerusalem leaders is a key power dynamic that operates in the accounts leading up to Jesus's death. Pilate is commonly perceived to be weak, letting the Jerusalem leaders force him into crucifying Jesus. But this is not accurate. Roman governors were not weak. Rather, Pilate knows that any enemy of his allies, the Jerusalem leaders, is his enemy. But he can't execute Jesus just because they demand it. That would make him look like their lackey.

Pilate gets the crowd to support his decision to crucify Jesus. He polls the crowd to see how much support Jesus has. He asks them what he should do with Jesus (Mark 15:9). Stirred up by the Jerusalem leaders, they shout for the release of the more popular Barabbas (15:11). He asks them about Jesus and his supposed crimes (15:12, 14). They demand crucifixion (15:13–14). He taunts the leaders and the crowd by saying he will not crucify Jesus. They, of course, beg him to do so (15:14b). Now he has them right where he wants them—dependent on him, begging him to use his power, subservient to him, while he *seems* to do *their* will (15:15).

Pilate is not weak and indecisive, but he is clever. Pilate is going to crucify Jesus anyway. With his questions, he has found out how much support Jesus has, and he has gained the crowd's support for crucifying a rebel king. It's a fine day's work by Pilate.

Eschatological Threats

In challenging Rome's power, Jesus does not, like most of the other rebels we have discussed above, resort to violence. And while he has followers (just like other rebel leaders), he prohibits his followers from using violence: "Do not resist an evildoer violently" (Matt. 5:39 my trans.). Why does Jesus renounce and forbid violence?

Part of the explanation has to do with the eschatological, or end-time, horizon for Jesus's teaching. Jesus was an eschatological prophet. While he announces that the reign or empire of God is present in his teaching and activity, he also announces that its completion lies in the future, in God's further intervention. He works with two temporal poles, the now and the not yet. *Now, already*, God's empire, God's rule, is active in his ministry. *Not yet*, though, are God's purposes accomplished in full. The time is coming, Jesus says, when God's purposes, God's reign, will be established in full.

A cluster of events composes this establishment. One event involves Jesus's return to earth as the agent of God's rule. He draws on the announcement of Daniel 7 to identify himself as the Son of Man who represents God's rule (Mark 14:62; Matt. 26:64). In Daniel 7, this rule follows God's judgment on the empires of the world. This is not, then, good news for Rome's empire and its allies. It is the end of the imperial world as they know it, the loss of their power and privileges. Jesus as God's agent claims to accomplish it. It's easy to kill the messenger when this is the message!

Another event involves the judgment of the nations. Jesus describes a scene in which at his coming as Son of Man he gathers all the nations and separates them, "as a shepherd separates the sheep from the goats" (Matt. 25:32). The criterion for receiving God's blessing concerns whether the nations have provided for the hungry, the thirsty, the stranger, the sick, the naked, and the imprisoned. These folks are commonly the casualties of empire, those who are deprived of adequate resources because imperial elites have become richer and more powerful at their expense. The criterion in God's judgment is not about how much power, status, and wealth one has accumulated, or how many peoples one has subjugated, or how many enemies one has killed. These are the common marks of success for an empire and its rulers and "great men." Rather, Jesus says, active care for the vulnerable and the weak constitutes God's criterion. Neglect of the vulnerable in God's scheme means punishment. In this scene, Jesus declares the coming end of the world of those presently in power and God's imminent condemnation of that world. Ironically, violence in the present is not necessary when this sort of violent future awaits.

Any empire fears someone who will make a compelling case that human interactions should not be organized on the basis of a few having much and many having little. Empires fear someone declaring, "It does not have to be this way; there is another way that is better for everyone." Jesus made such a case. He pointed to an alternative way of shaping human community. The invested powers had too much to lose. They took him out by hanging him on a cross to die.[15]

Interpretations of Jesus's Crucifixion

When Jesus was crucified, he did not leave his followers a manual explaining his execution's significance. Nor was there a copy of a memo to Pilate saying, "Crucify Jesus and do the world a favor—he'll take your sins away." Rather, Jesus's followers had to work out its significance. For two thousand years, Jesus's followers have been making sense of Jesus's crucifixion. What is its significance? What does it mean? Such interpretation is always ongoing. One week, for example, the signboard outside a church I drive by each day on the way to school read, "The key to heaven was hung on a nail." That is not a Bible verse. It's a very contemporary interpretation of Jesus's crucifixion— with its own websites.

The Christian tradition is rich with many different perspectives on Jesus's crucifixion. Some parts of the Christian tradition have focused on only one view and neglected this diversity. An emphasis, for example, on Jesus's crucifixion as a sacrifice for sin has often eclipsed other interpretations.

The numerous interpretations in the New Testament attest how urgent the task was for the first Jesus-believers to come to grips with Jesus's "most pitiable of deaths" by crucifixion (Josephus, *J.W.* 7.203).[16] What meaning could they make of it? What significance did it have? What did it mean to live in the Roman Empire as a follower of one who was crucified as a rebel? As we saw in chapter 2, New Testament writers looked to the Scriptures to find

15. Why are Jesus's followers not crucified with him? This question has troubled historians. I suggest that two factors explain the lack of any action against followers. (1) After Pilate has polled the crowd and not found great support for Jesus (he's not as popular as Barabbas), Pilate decides that the execution of Jesus is sufficient as a deterrent. (2) Jesus and his followers have not committed any violent actions against the elites and their property. Pilate regards Jesus's actions in the temple, along with his verbal threats that the end of the world is near, as contained by his crucifixion.

16. *Josephus* (Thackeray).

language and images to borrow. They borrowed, for example, the pattern of the righteous sufferer found in lament psalms (such as Ps. 22) to make sense of what had happened to Jesus. They borrowed the notion of prophets faithful to God's purposes but rejected by the people's leaders (so Luke 13:33–34). These are just a couple of many understandings.

Paul

Paul interprets Jesus's crucifixion in different ways. One interpretation, in Roman 3:25, is that Jesus's crucifixion was a "sacrifice of atonement by his blood." The reference to "blood" evokes crucifixion and sacrifice. Paul uses a word for "sacrifice of atonement" that in the Septuagint refers to "the mercy seat," the lid of "the ark of the covenant" (Exod. 25:17–22; Lev. 16). Sacrificial blood was sprinkled on this place to represent the taking away of sin at the annual Day of Atonement (Lev. 16:13–16). Paul borrows the image but reinterprets it to explain Jesus's crucifixion as the "place" where sin is removed.

But how did we get from Jesus the crucified rebel to Jesus as the one whose death is a sacrifice that takes away sin? Interestingly, this same word "sacrifice of atonement" that Paul uses in Romans 3:25 appears in 4 Maccabees 17:22: "And through the blood of those devout ones and their death as *an atoning sacrifice*, divine Providence preserved Israel that previously had been mistreated" (emphasis added). Fourth Maccabees is found in the Apocrypha. It was written perhaps early in the first century CE, several decades before Paul writes his letters.

Fourth Maccabees belongs in the tradition of 1 and 2 Maccabees, which we discussed in the last chapter. Second Maccabees, you will recall, tells the story of an elderly Jewish man named Eleazar, seven brothers, and their mother, all of whom choose terrible martyrdom rather than obey the decree of Antiochus Epiphanes requiring them to abandon their faith (2 Macc. 6–7). Fourth Maccabees retells and elaborates that story. In 2 Maccabees, the martyrdoms are presented as *appeals* to God to show mercy to Israel by ending the punishment for their sins as experienced through the horrible suffering inflicted by Antiochus. Fourth Maccabees goes a step further. In 4 Maccabees 17:22, the martyrdoms are understood as "an atoning sacrifice" that takes away Israel's sin of not being faithful to the covenant and preserves the nation from Antiochus Epiphanes.

By using the same word as 4 Maccabees, Paul presents Jesus's death as a martyrdom, as the death of one who refused to yield to Roman power but witnessed to God's rule (empire). But his death was not just his own. It was not just about Jesus. Paul (and numerous other early Jesus-believers) came to understand Jesus's martyrdom as "for us." That little phrase "for us" is theologically very important. The theology is in the preposition "for." The preposition signifies a beneficial connection between Jesus's death and Jesus's believers. It understands Jesus's death as a death, like those of the martyrs of 2 and 4 Maccabees, that benefited others. That benefit was not just an appeal for God's mercy, as in 2 Maccabees. It was, as in 4 Maccabees (borrowing from Exodus and Leviticus), a sacrifice that took away sin.[17]

1 CORINTHIANS 1:23

In 1 Corinthians Paul presents a very different interpretation. He presents Jesus's crucifixion as the standard for evaluating all forms of human thinking and behaving. In 1 Corinthians 1:23 he declares, "We proclaim Christ crucified, a stumbling block to Jews and foolishness to Gentiles." This verse is part of a larger section of 1 Corinthians, 1:18–2:5, in which Paul writes about the meaning of the cross. He does so to address a situation of division among the Corinthian believers (1 Cor. 1:10–17). Some among them use sophisticated speech and cultured thinking to emphasize their elevated birth, status, wealth, and power. Underscoring this rhetoric is a worldview typical of more elite people in provincial cities of the empire: it asserts the privilege and superiority of a few over all the rest.

Part of Paul's response is to indicate that the cross discloses or reveals God's way of working in the world and the sort of world God intends. The revealer of God's purposes is "Christ crucified" (1:23). "Christ crucified" is the means of assessing all human behaviors. This statement assumes the revulsion that most people in Paul's world experienced in thinking about crucifixion as a shameful and pitiable form of execution. As we have seen, crucifixion is about the punishment and societal exclusion of the nobodies, the undesirables, and the dangerous.

In the crucifixion of Jesus, Paul says, God shows that social structures of privilege and power mean nothing in God's purposes. God's preferences run elsewhere. "God chose what is low and despised in the world" (1:28). There is nothing lower and more despised in Paul's world than a crucified person, yet God's gracious power is evident even there, especially there, in "Christ crucified." But this flouts all common sense, all accepted wisdom. God's ways of workings are, Paul argues, so unusual, so absurd, so out of step with conventional human and imperial patterns of asserting superiority, of establishing dominance, of looking out for our own interests, of recognizing accomplishment and rewarding success. The cross pulls the rug out from

17. Paul presents Jesus's death as a sacrifice in both 1 Cor. 5:7 and Rom. 8:32 (alluding to Abraham's readiness to sacrifice Isaac in Gen. 22:16).

under all those ways of being human. It is offensive, ridiculous, nonsensical, "a stumbling block to Jews, and foolishness to Gentiles" (1:23). That verse includes everyone: "Jews and Gentiles" was a way of saying "all of us."

Paul's interpretation of "Christ crucified" has very practical sociopolitical implications. Those among the Corinthian believers who think they are superior to others and who treat others as less than themselves must stop doing so. Paul points to "Christ crucified" and calls them to imagine and live out different social interactions, based on valuing all people, especially the so-called nobodies. "Christ crucified" means alternative ways of being human. It means inclusive and just forms of social interaction based on God's way of acting graciously to all. "God chose what is foolish. . . . God chose what is weak" (1 Cor. 1:27).

Galatians 3:13

In Galatians 3:13, Paul thinks about Jesus's crucifixion yet in another way. Paul says, "Christ redeemed us from the curse of the law by becoming a curse for us—for it is written, 'Cursed is everyone who hangs on a tree.'" The notion of "curse" as the absence of God's favor is crucial to understanding this verse. To say that someone is "cursed" is to declare that the person is beyond or outside God's favor and grace. The law was a blessing: it conveyed God's favor. To be without or outside the law was to lack God's favor. To be hung on a tree was, according to Deuteronomy 21:23, to be beyond God's favor.

Paul evokes this conventional thinking. He identifies the one "hung on the tree" as the crucified rebel Jesus, cursed, beyond God's favor, so it would seem. Paul again uses that little phrase "for us." Being cursed is not just Jesus's lot, it is also the lot of every person, Jew and gentile. Jesus becomes "a curse for us."

But then Paul turns it upside down. Another assumption is in play, that of the resurrection. Jesus did not stay crucified. God raised him from the dead. For Paul, that act of God shows that nothing or no one is beyond God's favor, nothing or no one is outside the reach of God's grace, nothing or no one escapes God's power. God's grace, God's favor, God's love, God's power extend everywhere, even as far as a supposedly cursed person hung on a cross. God has raised a cursed one to life. God colors outside the lines. God runs with scissors. God is not bound by conventional rules.

And why does this matter? Because, as Paul says in the next verse, the raising of a (supposedly) cursed and crucified one shows that God's blessing extends everywhere to everyone, to both Jew and gentile. And that means, for the Galatian believers, they do not need to take on Jewish identity by being circumcised.

Gospels: Matthew

The Gospels also offer extensive reflection on the significance of Jesus's crucifixion. As just one example, we notice the range of perspectives and interpretations that Matthew's account of the events leading up to Jesus's crucifixion offers (chap. 26).

- The opening verses of chapter 26 present Jesus as announcing again his imminent crucifixion (26:1–2; cf. 16:21; 17:22–23; 20:17–19). That is, his crucifixion is not a surprise, not a defeat by his enemies. God's purposes are being worked out. Jesus is in control.
- At 26:3 the scene and perspective change. The Jerusalem power group schemes to arrest and crucify Jesus. Jesus has challenged their vision of a hierarchical, unjust society (20:25–28). People like what they hear. He has influence. Jesus is crucified because he attacks the societal structures guarded by and benefiting the elites.
- Verses 6–13 offer a contrasting perspective. A woman (not one of the male disciples) anoints Jesus for burial, recognizing he dies in God's service.
- Verses 14–16 highlight another contrasting perspective. Jesus's crucifixion results from betrayal by one of his disciples: Judas. And Judas's motive? Money.
- Verses 17–30 use the Passover setting of Jesus's death to interpret its significance. Passover celebrates the deliverance of God's people from Egyptian power. Now in the context of Roman power, Jesus identifies his poured-out blood with forgiveness or release and points to the future, when God's kingdom/empire will be established in full over all evil, including Rome's unjust and harsh rule.
- After the prediction of Peter's failure (26:31–35, 69–75), Jesus remains faithful to God's purposes in Gethsemane (26:36–46).
- When Jesus is betrayed by Judas and arrested (26:47–56), he refuses violent resistance. He does not summon an army of heavenly beings (26:51–54). He declares that the events happen according to the Scriptures. The general reference—no specific Scriptures cited here—is another way of speaking about God's will.
- In 26:57–68, before the high priest Caiaphas, Jesus is accused of predicting the destruction and rebuilding of the temple. There is an ambiguity about the identity of the temple. It refers both to the Jerusalem temple and to Jesus himself. Talk of destroying the temple attacks the leaders' power base. In response to the question of whether he is God's agent (Messiah),

SOME OTHER NEW TESTAMENT REFERENCES

Other parts of the New Testament interpret Jesus's crucifixion in different ways:

- We noticed John's Gospel's extra emphasis on Jesus as King of the Judeans. John seems to present Jesus's lifting up on the cross as a coronation (John 19:13–21). His cross is his throne! Linked with resurrection and ascension, it reveals God's life-giving purposes.

- Paul in Philippians 2:7–8 borrows the common link between slavery and crucifixion by presenting Jesus as a slave (2:7) who is obedient to his master, God, in being crucified (2:8). Paradoxically, God then exalts him so that everybody "in heaven and on earth" acknowledges his lordship.

- The writer of Colossians presents the cross as a place of reconciliation (1:20).

- Colossians also sees the cross as a place of victory over "the rulers and authorities" (2:14–15). Just who these rulers and authorities might be has been disputed. Some see them as angelic beings, or as evil spirits, or as stars and planets, or as divinities who were understood to control human governments and rulers. If the latter option is in view, Christ the rebel defeats the powers behind the sociopolitical powers who crucified him, when God raises him in the resurrection. Verse 15b uses the image of the triumph, a victory parade in which a victorious general or emperor entered Rome, parading booty and captured prisoners. Ironically here in Colossians, the risen Christ parades the defeated powers, human and heavenly, that crucified him.

- Revelation introduces Jesus as "the ruler of the kings of the earth" (1:5), referring to his victory through resurrection over their crucifying power. This emphasis on victorious power continues in 5:5, where Jesus is presented as a lion. But in 5:6 this lion stunningly becomes "a Lamb standing as if it had been slaughtered." "Standing" represents the Lamb's (Jesus's) power through his having been raised by God. "As if slaughtered" represents his violent death by crucifixion at the hands of the Roman and Jerusalem alliance. His power over the kings of the earth does not come from violence but from his vulnerability in absorbing their violence in martyrdom.

Jesus answers by quoting Daniel 7, with its vision of God's ending the reign of the world's empires (Rome's!) and giving charge of God's rule to "the Son of Man," Jesus. The chief priest cries "Blasphemy!" But with its declaration of Rome's downfall, this blasphemy is treason.

Matthew 27 continues to offer interpretations of and perspectives on Jesus's crucifixion, including Jesus as the rebel "King of the Judeans" (my trans.), claiming unsanctioned power against Rome's rule. Chapter 28 gives an account of Jesus's resurrection. The limits of Rome's power are revealed. They can't keep Jesus, God's agent, dead. And God gives to Jesus, not Rome, "all authority in heaven and on earth" (28:18). The irony is, of course, that this vision of God's victory over all things looks very much like Rome's assertion of power over all the nations.

Conclusion

Our fifth event, ca. 30 CE, concerns the crucifixion of Jesus. Rome used crucifixion to remove undesirables such as violent criminals, rebellious slaves, and brigands or rebels who opposed Roman rule. Jesus's declarations about God's kingdom/empire, his conflicts with Rome's allies in the Jerusalem temple leadership, and his eschatological declarations—all resulted in his being crucified as one who was understood to threaten Roman rule. The New Testament writers interpret his crucifixion in numerous ways to show its significance for Jesus-believers.

The Writing
of the New Testament Texts
(ca. 50–ca. 130 CE)

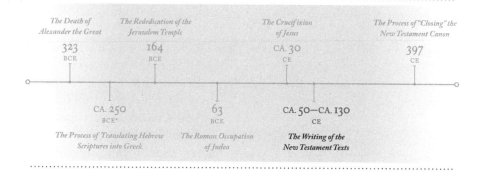

The Death of Alexander the Great	The Rededication of the Jerusalem Temple		The Crucifixion of Jesus		The Process of "Closing" the New Testament Canon
323 BCE	164 BCE		CA. 30 CE		397 CE
	CA. 250 BCE*	63 BCE	CA. 50—CA. 130 CE		
	The Process of Translating Hebrew Scriptures into Greek	The Roman Occupation of Judea	The Writing of the New Testament Texts		

Our focus in this chapter moves us forward some twenty years and more from Jesus's crucifixion in ca. 30 CE. Our sixth key event stretches the meaning of "event" quite a bit. This sixth event in fact spans eight decades from about 50 CE to about 130 CE. During these decades, the documents that will later form the New Testament are written. We do not know precisely when most of these documents that end up forming the New Testament were written, so we will need to keep in mind the *approximate* dimension of the 50–130 CE period. These decades, with their production of New Testament writings, were incredibly influential and formative for the emerging movement of Jesus-believers.

Referring to writings such as Paul's Letters or the four Gospels as "New Testament writings" seems natural to us in the twenty-first century. But it would have been very strange to anyone in the first and second centuries. There wasn't a New Testament then. There wasn't a committee planning one. How and why writings were gathered to form a definitive New Testament collection or canon will be the focus of the next chapter. So we will refer to them as New Testament writings in this chapter, recognizing that the description is anachronistic for the first and second centuries.

We begin this chapter by discussing Paul's Letters. Next we move to some of the writings composed after Paul's death. These writings include letters written in Paul's name (Ephesians, 1 and 2 Timothy) as well as the book of Acts, in which Paul is the hero. Then we discuss some of the other letters—or writings that include features of letters—such as 1 and 2 Peter, James, Hebrews, and Revelation. We finish with a fourth section, which discusses the Gospels. Through the chapter we think about the forms, functions, and content of the writings for communities of Jesus-believers.

Paul's Letters

Paul has always been a controversial figure. He was so in his own lifetime, and he has been so ever since. People have found much in his Letters to argue about. As the writer of 2 Peter says, some decades after Paul, "There are some things in [Paul's Letters] hard to understand, which the ignorant and

unstable twist to their own destruction" (2 Pet. 3:16). Yes, Paul is hard to understand; the eschatological framework of his thinking, his vocabulary, his sophisticated arguments, and the specific but often elusive (for us) situations he addresses make him difficult. But labeling those who disagree with your interpretation of Paul as "ignorant and unstable" doesn't help much.

Starting our discussion with Paul's Letters might seem strange given that the Gospels come first in the New Testament canon. But there is a good reason. Paul's

Figure 6.1. Paul writing (Wuselig/Wikimedia Commons)

THE FORM OF LETTERS

Letters in Paul's world followed something of a predictable form. They begin with the salutation, which identifies the sender and the recipient, and in which the writer greets the addressee. A thanksgiving or prayer follows that acknowledges the relationship and often focuses on the recipient's health. Then comes the body of the letter, in which the main content is covered. The conclusion can include a number of elements, depending on the letter: final commands, the wishing of peace, final greetings from or to shared acquaintances, a closing benediction.

Paul does his theological-pastoral work by using and adapting this form. In the salutation, he names himself, but he can also introduce or define himself at length. In Romans 1:1–6, writing to a church he did not begin, the lengthy self-identification functions to introduce him to them, reassure them, and sum up his understanding of his gospel. His greetings usually include "grace and peace," two terms that are rich with theological meaning in relation to God's purposes. The thanksgivings allow Paul to introduce significant matters that he will expand in the letter.

We see this in the thanksgiving in 1 Corinthians. Paul highlights the readers' spiritual gifts (1:7), a topic he will provide further instruction about in chapters 12–14. He also refers to the future "day of our Lord Jesus Christ" (1:7–8). This "day" refers to the future completion of God's purposes, which he will elaborate in 1 Corinthians 15 when he corrects those in Corinth who think that already God's purposes are completed (see 4:8).

Yet in one letter he does not give thanks. In Galatians he seems to be so aggravated with the Galatians' reception of other teachers that he skips the thanksgiving pleasantries and begins: "I am astonished that you are so quickly deserting the one who called you in the grace of Christ and are turning to a different gospel" (1:6).

The body of his letters includes theological, ethical, and ecclesiological instruction. And he finishes with the same array of closing elements, but shapes them so as to express his theological message. The conclusion of 2 Corinthians, for example, includes a quick-fire list of final commands (13:11), a call for a holy kiss (v. 12), greetings from other believers (v. 13), and a benediction (v. 14).

Letters were written before the Gospels. They are the earliest writings we have from the emerging Jesus movement. The order in which writings were placed in the canon does not reflect the chronological order in which they were written. So we start with Paul's Letters because they were the earliest of the New Testament writings.

Composite Letters?

Some have wondered if several of Paul's Letters as we have them now might be composite letters, each composed by combining parts of several letters to make one letter. In 2 Corinthians, there is a significant change in tone and emphasis between chapters 1–9 and 10–13. How do we explain this change? Did Paul get interrupted by changing circumstances? Did he not have strong-enough coffee one morning? Did the bedbugs bite? Or were parts of two separate letters combined later on? Likewise, some scholars have sought to explain changes of tone and content in Philippians by suggesting that our Philippians might comprise pieces from three separate letters, with 4:10–20 and chapter 3 being two of the pieces.

In writing letters, Paul borrowed a common form of communication from his pre-email, pre-texting, pre-tweeting cultural world. How many letters Paul wrote is not clear. In the New Testament, thirteen letters carry his name as writer. Most scholars, though, think that Paul wrote only seven of these thirteen (Romans, 1 and 2 Corinthians, Galatians, Philippians, 1 Thessalonians, Philemon), while followers or disciples of Paul wrote the other six, using his esteemed name (Ephesians, Colossians, 2 Thessalonians, 1 and 2 Timothy, Titus). We accept this division for the time being and later return to discuss some of the reasons for and implications of it. It might also be helpful to say at this point that recognizing this division of letters written or not written by Paul does not mean that these six letters are to be disregarded.

So Paul wrote at least seven letters. But that's not the end of the story. In both 1 and 2 Corinthians, he mentions other letters he has written to the Corinthians. In 1 Corinthians 5:9–10 he refers to one such letter, which they seem to have misunderstood: "I wrote to you in my letter not to associate with sexually immoral persons—not at all meaning . . . But now I am writing to you . . ." This reference to a previous letter indicates that our 1 Corinthians is actually 2 Corinthians!

A similar thing happens in our 2 Corinthians. Written perhaps a couple of years after 1 Corinthians, 2 Corinthians 2:3–4 refers to another letter that Paul has written. "And I wrote as I did, so that when I came, I might not suffer pain from those who should have made me rejoice. . . . For I wrote you out of much distress and anguish of heart and with many tears, not to cause you pain, but to let you know the abundant love that I have for you." It would not be accurate to describe 1 Corinthians as showing such great "distress" and "anguish of heart," so Paul must be referring to another letter. The letter he references here would make 2 Corinthians actually 4 Corinthians! These two letters referred to in 1 Corinthians 5:9–10 and 2 Corinthians 2:3–4 have not survived as far as we know. Given Paul's descriptions of these two letters—one misunderstood and one causing much pain—it is no surprise that the Corinthians did not treasure them enough to keep them! Did Paul write other letters that did not survive, to other churches?

Local Contexts

Noticing these other letters Paul wrote highlights the key role that context plays in understanding Paul's Letters. The letters are not isolated, "one-off," free-floating communications. He doesn't write a general letter and send it off to everyone on his contacts list. Rather, the letters are part of an evolving relationship between Paul and the believing communities, and they are tied to the specific circumstances that they address. Thus 1 and 2 Corinthians provide evidence for Paul's evolving relationship and extended interactions with these communities of believers. Before writing 1 Corinthians, for example, Paul has

- been in Corinth to found the community (1 Cor. 4:15);
- written them a letter (5:9–11);
- received visits from some of the Corinthian believers: Chloe's people (1:11); Fortunatus, Stephanas, Achaicus (16:17–18); some reporters (5:1);

Figure 6.2. Corinth (MM/Wikimedia Commons)

- received a letter from them (7:1);
- and sent Timothy to visit them (4:17–18).

Then he writes 1 Corinthians, in which he responds to some of the issues they have raised. He regularly uses the phrase "now concerning" to introduce some of these issues (7:1; 8:1; 12:1; 16:1).

Interactions between Paul and the Corinthian believers continue after this letter.

- Paul makes another visit to Corinth, which does not go well. He calls it a "painful visit" (2 Cor. 2:1).
- He writes them a tearful or sorrowful letter (2:2–4).
- He seems to send the letter with Titus (rather than taking it himself: 1:23; 2:1).
- Titus achieves some reconciliation, which pleases Paul (7:5–16).
- Other teachers have been welcomed into the community. They have raised doubts about Paul's legitimacy and integrity (2 Cor. 12; 13:3), which does not please Paul (2 Cor. 10–13).
- Paul writes 2 Corinthians.

In this sequence of interactions, Paul's Letters function as surrogates for his presence. When he can't be there or when he deems it wiser not to be there, he sends a letter. Through his letters, he does his ministry of pastoral care, of proclamation and instruction, of encouragement and rebuke, of checking up and checking in. Yet we always get only Paul's side of the story in these letters. Reading them is like listening to one end of a telephone conversation and trying to imagine who the other person is and what that person is saying.

In reading Paul's Letters as part of the New Testament canon, it is easy for us to neglect these sequences of interactions. It is easy to get the false impression that Paul's voice is the only voice as he single-handedly runs around the empire, founding and instructing churches. But on closer examination, it is clear that there are many voices and personalities in these communities. Various voices compete for influence. The selection of Paul's Letters for the canon elevates Paul's voice and silences others, often rendering them invisible. Yet it is clear that there were not only numerous voices but also lots of conflict in these communities.

In 1 Corinthians, for example, the Corinthians do not get along with one another (11:19). There are factions committed to different apostles (1:11–12). There seem to be a few wealthier, more elite people, perhaps patrons in the church, and many poorer folks (1:26–29). Divisions between the haves and the have-nots are very apparent at the church potlucks and celebrations of the Lord's Supper, where some have plenty to eat and drink while others have little (11:17–34). There seem to be some who think they are spiritually superior to everyone else and already enjoy the fullness of God's purposes (1:18–2:16; 4:8–10; chaps. 12–14). In chapter 9 some do not seem to get along with Paul. Various contentious practices have developed among the Corinthians, and Paul weighs in with instructions about sex (chap. 5); lawsuits among believers (chap. 6); spirituality, sex, and marriage (chap. 7); food offered to idols (chaps. 8–10); and worship (chaps. 11–14). He is clearly one voice among many.

In 2 Corinthians some other figures have come among the community and have challenged Paul's authority and right to speak. The conflict, as he unfolds it—and we have only his side of the story—concerns the criteria that mark a true leader or "apostle" among the believing communities (2 Cor. 12:12; 13:3). Today, denominations have very clearly defined processes through which candidates for ministry are evaluated and credentialed (ordained). But in the 50s CE, this was not so. How does one recognize a true apostle or reliable preacher in these believing communities?

According to Paul, it's all about knowing the right criteria. He disparagingly labels these others teachers "superapostles" (2 Cor. 11:5), and then calls them "false apostles, deceitful workers, disguising themselves as apostles of Christ" and claims that they are actually servants of Satan (2 Cor. 11:13–15). This very abusive language suggests that the conflict is intense, emotions are high, and much is on the line. He goes on to discuss various appeals to the criteria by which they commend themselves: superior skill in speech (10:10; 11:6), comparisons with others (10:12), claiming financial support (11:7–12), showing greater love (11:11; 12:15), being more faithful to their Jewish heritage and ministry in Christ (11:22–23), and having superior spiritual experiences (12:1–10).

Paul's response is that they boast or commend themselves according to human or cultural standards of their day (11:18). These criteria were the sorts of things philosophers and traveling teachers used in the Greco-Roman world. They are cultural and worldly criteria. Paul responds by saying that he can more than match these "false apostles" by these criteria. Anything they can do, he can do better, he says. But he is adamant that God does not play by these rules (10:18). God's commendation does not depend on these cultural criteria. It has an altogether different basis.

So Paul defends himself against what seem to be accusations made against him: "The signs of a true apostle were performed among you" (2 Cor. 12:12) he declares. And again he defends himself: "since you desire proof that Christ is speaking in me" (13:3). And his criterion: he lives the gospel in human weakness and divine power. He lives the Gospel pattern of crucifixion and resurrection (13:3b–4). Paul testifies to having a "thorn in the flesh"—and no one knows what he is referring to—that he asked God to remove. God did not remove "it"; instead, Paul learned that God's "power is made perfect in weakness," that "the power of Christ may dwell" in him in weakness (12:9). His ultimate defense here is that he lives the gospel of the crucified and risen Jesus, the same gospel that he preaches.

Paul seems defensive, touchy, and irascible in 2 Corinthians. He is, of course, fighting for his integrity and his ministry, so there is much on the line. But the significant thing to observe is that there is no agreement among Paul, the other teachers, and the Corinthians as to the rules for the fight. There is no agreement as to how one recognizes "the signs of a true apostle" (12:12). How do they recognize a faithful apostle or teacher through whom God is speaking? The other teachers claim legitimacy by presenting themselves in terms of everyday cultural standards. Paul says that's the wrong game and the wrong rules. Instead, he says, the only basis for discerning a true spokesperson and teacher is whether the teacher walks the talk of the gospel in terms of weakness and power, crucifixion and resurrection (4:7–12). The Corinthians, or at least some of them, seem drawn to the other teachers.

Highlighting these contexts of changing circumstances, many voices, and conflict provides insight into how Paul does his pastoral and teaching work. One thing is clear: he takes very seriously the circumstances he is addressing. Paul does not have just one letter that he texts all over the empire. He does not say in 2 Corinthians, for example, "Hi, folks: See my previous letter. Love, Paul." He writes a new letter to address new and different circumstances. Nor does he say to the church in Rome, "I wrote this very fine letter to the church in Corinth last week—just sending it along. Love, Paul."

Doing Ministry

Such an approach, though, raises a question about how Paul does his ministry in these changing circumstances. Does he say whatever he thinks meets the different situations that arise? Or does he speak to the situations out of a set of consistent theological convictions? Are his letters a random collection of spur-of-the-moment advice, or do they translate a set of consistent and core convictions that frame his teaching for different circumstances?

A few scholars have suggested that Paul's Letters do not offer a cohesive theological understanding. Most interpreters, though, understand Paul to be at least a somewhat coherent theological thinker, with some central convictions—his gospel—informing what he says to the changing circumstances of specific churches (at least as he understands them). There has been, though, much debate about what elements might compose this coherent center or unifying content.

An older approach, which ultimately derives from the sixteenth-century Protestant Reformation, sees "justification" at the center of Paul's theology. When God "justifies the ungodly" (Rom. 4:5), God declares people forgiven of sin and sets them in right relationship with God because of Jesus's death on the cross. But the problem with this suggested center is that while Paul uses justification language in Romans and Galatians, it does not figure much elsewhere in his letters. And it is not the only image or metaphor he uses in Romans and Galatians to picture God's activity (e.g., "reconciliation" in Rom. 5:10–11; "adoption" in Rom. 8:15–24).

A second suggested center for Paul's theological thinking has focused on the phrase "in Christ."[1] Paul uses this common phrase in relation to (a) salvation through Jesus's death and resurrection (Rom. 6:3–4), (b) the community created by Christ's death and resurrection (the church, Rom. 12:5), and (c) ethical living that results from this identification (2 Cor. 2:17). Clearly it is an important phrase, but it does not embrace some aspects of Paul's thought. While it focuses on the past and present of being in Christ, it neglects important future dimensions. While it focuses on Christ, it neglects God's role and the Spirit's role. And while it focuses on the church, it neglects the ongoing role of Israel in Paul's thinking (cf. Rom. 9–11).

A third approach has identified a larger framework for Paul's theological thinking.[2] This approach sees Paul as a more theocentric (God-centered) and future-oriented (eschatological) thinker. It highlights four big themes:

- *Vindication* emphasizes that the death, resurrection, and yet-future return of Jesus display God's faithfulness to God's promises to redeem all of creation (Rom. 3:1–5; 1 Cor. 15:20–28).
- *Universalism* recognizes that in Jesus, God acts for all people, Jew and gentile, male and female (no male privilege through circumcision), and for all creation (Gal. 3:28; Rom. 8:18–25).
- *Dualism* recognizes that Paul is an eschatological thinker in that he understands there to be two ages or eras, the present one under the power of sin and a future one under God's purposes (Gal. 1:3–4). This, then,

---

1. E. P. Sanders, *Paul and Palestinian Judaism* (Philadelphia: Fortress, 1977), 431–74.
2. J. C. Beker, *Paul's Apocalyptic Gospel: The Coming Triumph of God* (Philadelphia: Fortress, 1982).

PAUL DOING MINISTRY AND THEOLOGY

What does this interplay between contingency and coherency, between circumstances and theological convictions, look like? In 1 Corinthians much of the discussion focuses on particular circumstances, as we have noted. In chapter 15, however, Paul elaborates some of his underlying theological convictions in presenting Jesus's resurrection as the "firstfruits," or guarantee, of the future general resurrection, which will embrace all of God's material creation, including human bodies (15:20–28). In affirming somatic or bodily resurrection (15:35–58), Paul emphasizes that life in bodies matters in God's purposes now and in the future resurrection. The Corinthians need to assess how they relate to one another and how they live in the light of these divine purposes that are under way but not yet complete. The themes of vindication (God will complete God's purposes), universalism (all of human existence and all of creation are involved), dualism (God's purposes are under way but not yet completed), and imminence (anytime now Jesus will return, and God will complete God's work) are evident.

is a temporal dualism. In the death and resurrection of Jesus, God has already, in part, broken into the present age so that the new era of God's reign is under way, but it is not yet established in full (Rom. 5:12–21).

• *Imminence* recognizes Paul's expectation that any time now, at a time that no one knows, Jesus will return to complete God's purposes by establishing God's reign over all. Jesus's return is necessary because not yet is the fullness of God's purpose established. In the meantime, in the overlap of the ages, Jesus-believers live and work in solidarity with a suffering creation that yearns for redemption, and in hope for God's certain and sure completion of God's good and life-giving purposes (1 Thess. 4:13–5:11).

This approach sees Paul as doing his theology and ministry in an interplay of contingency (circumstances) and coherency (his understanding of the gospel embraced by these four large themes).

Most scholars date Paul's seven surviving letters to (perhaps) the late 40s CE and (mostly) to the decade of the 50s, some twenty or so years after Jesus's crucifixion. We do not know, though, when or how Paul died. Some traditions say he was killed in 64 CE, when the emperor Nero blamed Jesus-believers in Rome for a fire that he himself probably lit. But this is a later tradition, and its historical value is somewhat unclear.

After Paul's Death: WWPS?

Whatever the circumstances of Paul's death, he certainly had a productive literary afterlife. That is, even when he had been long dead, stories featuring Paul emerged, such as the book of Acts (the 90s–120s CE) and *The Acts of Paul and Thecla* (second century CE). And people attributed writings to him that he clearly did not write. For example, there is an exchange of letters attributed to Paul and the Roman philosopher Seneca, probably written in the fourth century, centuries after the death of both!

The New Testament contains six letters attributed to Paul that he probably did not write. These letters are Ephesians, Colossians, 2 Thessalonians, 1 and 2 Timothy, and Titus. They were probably written late in the first century CE by some followers of Paul in the generation or two after Paul died (though some scholars dispute this). It was quite common in the ancient world for disciples of an important thinker or key figure to attribute writings to their teacher long dead. This practice was not an attempt to deceive with forgeries. Rather it was seen partly as a way of honoring the teacher and keeping alive the tradition of teaching. But especially, it was a way of addressing the question of relevance. How could the teachings of an important teacher address the different circumstances of later generations? If Paul were here, WWPS (What would Paul say)?

The determination that Paul probably did not write these letters is not just a modern one. The second-century character Marcion, who was a huge fan of Paul, did not include the Letters of Timothy and Titus (often called the Pastoral Epistles) in his list of Paul's writings. So how do scholars decide whether Paul wrote these documents?

Usually four factors are involved in determining whether Paul wrote these letters. The first three—vocabulary, style, historical circumstances—are not very conclusive, in my view. They provide data that *might* point to different authors, but they do not provide a compelling argument for this conclusion (see the sidebar "Factors Determining Authorship").

More compelling are the significant differences in theological understandings. These six letters reformulate significant aspects of Paul's thinking. It certainly is possible for Paul to change his mind, but these letters suggest more than a change of mind. They offer a major reworking of Paul's thought, a significantly different understanding of God's activity, even while they use Paul's language. Same words, different meanings.

One significant reorientation concerns the church. In Paul's Letters, the church is a local community of believers, struggling with issues like relationships, leadership, authority, and the imperial world of which it is a part. In

Factors Determining Authorship

The first two factors—vocabulary and style—require good knowledge of Greek, the language in which the letters are written (thanks, Alexander!). Scholars count the words across all the letters and compare where clusters of words appear. For example, one-third of the 900 words or so in the Pastorals (1 and 2 Timothy and Titus) do not appear elsewhere in writings linked with Paul. They are not words Paul typically uses to express himself. Also, 175 of their words do not appear elsewhere in the New Testament, and 211 are words commonly used in various second-century writings. These clusters suggest to some that these letters were written early in the second century, well after Paul's death.

Likewise there are some differences in style. These features are sometimes hard to notice in English translations. Paul at times uses a question-and-answer technique and short sentences, but both of these stylistic features are not typical of these six writings.

What are we to make of these observations? Certainly they highlight some important differences. But are the writing samples big enough for comparisons and meaningful conclusions? Moreover, the differences could be explained in various ways, such as different subject matter and changing situations. They *could*, but do not necessarily, point to a different author.

It is the same with the third factor, concerning the circumstances of the letters. Scholars argue about where in the circumstances of Paul's life these letters might belong. A chronology of Paul's life is very hard to formulate because we do not have a lot of information. And as we have seen, Paul's Letters are addressed to specific situations, whereas these six letters seem to be much more general. But again, these are difficult questions to settle with the limited information we have, and they can be explained in different ways.

1 Corinthians 12, the issue concerns how to use everyone's gifts; Romans 12 emphasizes relationships and love; Galatians concerns (in part) whether gentiles need to be circumcised to belong to this group. In contrast to this focus on local communities of Jesus-believers is Ephesians' cosmic presentation. The church is a cosmic entity. It exists "in the heavenly places," it is the "body" of the risen Christ, it is "the fullness of him who fills all in all" (Eph. 1:3, 22–23). This is a very different, cosmic understanding of the church.

Also different is the relationship between the present and the future in understanding God's work of salvation. In Ephesians, for example, believers have *already* received in the present "every spiritual blessing" (1:3). Christ has *already* been "seated at [God's] right hand in the heavenly places, far above all rule and authority and power and dominion, . . . and [God] has put all things under his feet" (1:20–22). Believers have *already* been "raised up with him and seated with him in the heavenly places in Christ Jesus" (2:6). The unity of Jew and gentile has *already* been accomplished (2:16). The keyword here, in case you hadn't noticed, is "already." *Already* believers experience the fullness of God's purposes according to Ephesians.

This focus on what has *already* been accomplished in the present, however, is not Paul's emphasis. Some of the believers in Corinth seem to have claimed similar things, and Paul strongly opposes them (1 Cor. 4:8–10). For Paul, these things—establishing and experiencing the fullness of God's purposes—have not yet taken place. These things remain in the future, to be accomplished when God completes God's purposes. So in Romans 6:4–5, the raising of believers with Christ remains future, as the future tense indicates: "We *will* certainly be united with him in a resurrection like his" (emphasis added). In 1 Corinthians 15:20–28, only at "the end" (15:24), after Christ's coming, will Christ rule over all rulers and have all things "in subjection under his feet" (15:24–27). Only in the future will Jew and gentile be fully reconciled in the mercy of God (Rom. 11:25–32). According to Paul, God's coming triumph will accomplish all these things in the future. Ephesians, however, offers a major reformulation of Paul's theology by moving future acts into the present, by declaring what Paul says will be done in the future as already accomplished.

Significant reformulations of Paul's thinking occur also in the Pastorals. These letters use some words that are important for Paul but provide those terms with new meanings. Paul's word "faith," for example, expresses a dynamic relationship with God marked by trust, dependence, obedience, and hope; in the Pastorals it comes to mean "the faith" in the sense of a body of doctrine (1 Tim. 3:9). The word "righteousness," which for Paul signifies "the power of God for salvation" (Rom. 1:16–17), becomes a moral quality of right living (1 Tim. 6:11). The church, which for Paul is structured by gifts of the Spirit (1 Cor. 12–14), becomes an institution with hierarchical and fixed offices (1 Tim. 3:1–13). Women, who share with Paul all the "work" of the gospel, including church planting and teaching (Rom. 16:1–7), in the Pastorals are to be silent and submissive to men, and to bear children (1 Tim. 2:11–15). Generally these six letters imitate the male-dominant patterns of households in their society, according to which husbands and males are leaders, and women and slaves submit obediently in domestic contexts (Eph. 5:21–6:9; Col. 3:18–4:1; 1 Tim. 3:1–13; 5:1–6). While Paul does not consistently resist this dominant patriarchal pattern, he does challenge it to some extent in imagining communities in which gender roles are equal (Gal. 3:28),[3] and in treating women like Phoebe and Prisca as equal coworkers (Rom. 16:1–3).

The very different theological and ecclesial formulations found in these six letters indicate that Paul probably did not write them. The decrease in focus on the future and the accommodation to cultural patterns dominant in society suggest that they were written a generation or two after Paul. There are new circumstances. Jesus has not returned. The church seems to be settling in for the long haul. The letters address this new situation. They assist the church in establishing structures, becoming more institutionalized, consolidating its beliefs, establishing boundaries with outsiders, and exhorting believers to moral living. In these six letters, followers of Paul reinterpret his message for these new circumstances. The New Testament includes these quite diverse theological understandings.

The book of Acts does a similar reinterpretation in its presentation of Paul as the hero of its story. Paul doesn't write any letters in Acts; he is a missionary. Acts is written either late in the first century or in the first few decades of the second century. Its big agenda concerns the inclusion of gentile believers in God's purposes. The mission to gentiles is shown from the outset to be God's good idea.

In the opening chapter, the risen Jesus tells the disciples to remain in Jerusalem: "But you will receive power when the Holy Spirit has come upon you; and you will be my witnesses in Jerusalem, in all Judea and Samaria, and to the ends of the earth" (Acts 1:8). Disciples are to bear witness in three geographical locations: (1) Jerusalem, (2) all Judea and Samaria, and (3) to the ends of the earth. The risen Jesus not only promises them power through the Holy Spirit and appoints them to a worldwide mission; he also provides a plot summary and outline of the structure of the book of Acts based on this geographical pattern. Chapters 1–7 focus on the believers in Jerusalem. In chapter 8, "a severe persecution" scatters the believers into Judea and Samaria (8:1). Chapters 9–28 narrate the mission to the gentiles. This expansion among the nations carries out the risen Jesus's plan outlined in 1:8.

The primary agent of this gentile mission is Paul. Acts presents Paul as *the* missionary who brings the gospel to the gentiles and who suffers in the process. The third section (Acts 9–28) begins with the risen Jesus's calling Paul to "bring [his] name before Gentiles and kings and before the people of Israel" (9:15). Twice more, in chapters 22 and 26, accounts of Paul's call are

3. See Elisabeth Schüssler Fiorenza, *In Memory of Her: A Feminist Theological Construction of Christian Origins* (New York: Crossroads, 1983); Carolyn Osiek and Margaret Y. MacDonald with Janet H. Tulloch, *A Woman's Place: House Churches in Earliest Christianity* (Minneapolis: Fortress, 2006).

provided, emphasizing that Paul will be "[Jesus's] witness to all the world" (22:15), that the risen Jesus "will send [Paul] far away to the Gentiles" (22:21; 26:17, 20). At least six times in these three accounts, God, or the risen Jesus, asserts Paul's identity and role as *the* missionary to gentiles. If something is repeated this many times, it must be important. If something is repeated, it must be important. If something is repeated, it . . .

In chapters 10–11 attention moves to the crucial encounter between Peter and the gentile Cornelius. The narrative is full of references to angels (Acts 10:3–7; 11:13), visions (10:11; 11:5), divine voices (10:13–16; 11:7–9), the Spirit (10:19, 44–48; 11:12, 15), God (10:28; 11:17), and the Lord (10:33). Divine guidance, intervention, and interpretation mark the narrative. The gentile mission is God's work.

In the next few chapters, Peter phases out of the action, and increasingly Paul comes to the fore as *the* missionary to the gentiles. In Acts 13, he preaches in the city of Antioch in Pisidia, applying the words of Isaiah 49:6 to himself, that "the Lord has commanded us, saying, 'I have set you to be a light for the gentiles, so that you may bring salvation to the ends of the earth'" (13:47). The second half of Acts presents Paul as the missionary hero, resolutely carrying out the God-sanctioned gentile mission. Throughout he suffers very much. Constantly his preaching is opposed through attempted stonings (14:5–6, 19–20), dissention and disagreements (15:5, 36–40), violent crowds and riots (16:19; 17:5–9; 19:21–41; 21:27–36), beatings (16:22–24), arrest (21:30), and imprisonments (16:23–34; chaps. 21–28). Throughout he is sustained and directed in his preaching and teaching of the churches by divine assurances (16:10; 18:9–10; 22:21; 23:11).

Acts presents Paul as faithful to his commission from the risen Jesus, even to "the ends of the earth" (1:8). He completes his mission in that he eventually can "bear witness also in Rome," the center of the Roman Empire (23:11). Acts finishes with Paul under house arrest in Rome, proclaiming "this salvation of God . . . to the Gentiles" (28:28).

But in contrast to Paul's Letters, a strange thing happens along the way. The Paul of Acts, though commissioned to be the missionary to the gentiles, usually visits Jewish communities first (Acts 16:11–15; 17:1–4). In the Acts narrative, a few members of these communities believe, but usually most reject him and the gospel. This pattern does not hold out much hope for including Jewish people in God's purposes. But this is the exact opposite of what Paul says in Romans 11. There he is quite confident that "all Israel will be saved" (11:26), quite sure that "God has imprisoned all in disobedience so that God may be merciful to all" (11:32). All means all. Paul gets a makeover in Acts.

Other Letters

Letters are not only ascribed to Paul after his death. The New Testament
also includes letters associated with Peter, John, and James. Because of space
limits, we cannot discuss all these letters. We will have to pass over the three
letters written in John's name, and the Letter of Jude.

The two letters written in Peter's name were probably composed after Peter's
death, traditionally understood to have occurred in the 60s CE during Nero's
attack on believers in Rome. The sophisticated Greek of 1 Peter and reference
in 2 Peter to a previous generation of apostles (3:2) probably rule out Peter as
the author of either letter, even though they evoke his name and authority to
honor him and make apparent autobiographical references (1 Pet. 5:1; 2 Pet.
1:16–18). Some think 2 Peter may be the latest writing in the New Testament,
from about the 120s to 130s CE.

First Peter. Perhaps written from Rome, this letter addresses believers in
the provinces in the northern part of Asia Minor (Turkey today). It exhorts
them to faithful living as followers of Jesus. So it begins by outlining their
identity in God's merciful purposes (1:3–12) before calling them to live holy,
obedient, virtuous, and faithful lives (1:13–4:19). Earning a good reputation
with gentiles (2:12–17) and imitating or participating in the sufferings of
Jesus (chap. 3; 4:12–19) are important motivations. The letter unfortunately
assumes and maintains slavery (2:18–25) and the subordinate roles of women
(3:1–7). It closes by exhorting elders, presumably leaders in the assemblies, to
be faithful in their responsibilities for "the flock of God" (5:1–11).

Second Peter. The author of this letter presents himself as "Simeon Peter"
(1:1a) and as near death (1:12–15). He writes a kind of farewell letter to an
unspecified audience (1:1b) to "remind" them of matters basic to their faith
(1:12). The writer is concerned about false teachers emerging among them (2:1)
and, using conventional terms, spends most of chapter 2 describing their false
strategies and practices. He assures his audience that God will bring about
the false teachers' destruction and ensure their safety and salvation with God
(2:9). It seems that the false teachers especially mock the notion of the second
coming of Jesus (3:4). In response, the author reminds his audience of God's
faithfulness (3:9–10) and urges them to live in holy and godly expectancy as
they await the coming of Jesus and completion of God's purposes (3:11–18).

James. Like 2 Peter, this letter is written to a general audience by an important leader. Whether James the brother of Jesus and leader of the Jerusalem
church until his death in 62 CE is the actual author is not clear. The letter
does not reflect his concern with faithfulness to the Torah, nor does it directly
refer to Jesus's life, death, resurrection, or return. The name Jesus appears

only twice, in 1:1 and 2:1. The letter is very concerned with the lowly poor (1:9), including widows and orphans (1:27), who are part of the assembly of believers (2:2) and dependent on alms for basic necessities (2:14–17). It particularly attacks the rich (1:10) who display their wealth (2:2), oppress the poor (2:5–7), arrogantly assume they can secure their own lives (4:13–17), and face God's judgment (5:1–6). The book exhorts active discipleship in facing trials (1:2–4, 12–16), asking God for wisdom (1:5–8), being doers of the word (1:19–27; 2:14–26), loving neighbors impartially and practically (2:1–13), speaking well (3:1–12; 4:11–12), submitting to God rather than being friends with the world (4:1–10), enduring faithfully until Jesus returns (5:7–12), and praying faithfully (5:13–20).

Hebrews. This book describes itself as a "word of exhortation" (13:22). Who is being exhorted is not clear: Does it address Jewish and/or gentile readers? The letter does hint at some circumstances that it addresses: some have not made good progress to maturity (5:11–12), some have fallen away from their initial commitment to Christ (6:4–6), some face difficult and oppositional circumstances that challenge their commitment to Christ (10:32–36), and some risk growing "weary or losing heart" and might perhaps return to Judaism (12:3). The document largely alternates sections of teaching with sections of exhortations. Much of the explanation draws on Scriptures from the Hebrew Bible—especially the Psalms, the Pentateuch, and the Prophets—and reads them in relation to Jesus, who is God's Son (chap. 3), high priest (chaps. 4–5), mediator of a new covenant (chap. 8), and sacrifice (chaps. 9–10).

Revelation. The opening verses of this mysterious book identify three genres. It is an "apocalypse," or revelation, of God's purposes manifested in Jesus (1:1–2). It is a prophecy, or foretelling, of those purposes (1:3). And it is a letter that addresses those revelations to seven churches in the province of Asia (1:4–5, 20; chaps. 2–3). What does Revelation reveal?[4]

The opening chapter reveals something about itself, its claim to be God's Word for God's world. The chapter presents the risen Christ, "the faithful witness, the firstborn of the dead, and the ruler of the kings of the earth" (1:5), as the means of the divine revelation that John passes on. The revelation of God's purposes is addressed to seven churches in Asia in chapters 2–3. In seven short letters, these chapters commend these churches as well as rebuke them. The key revelation to them is that the Jesus-believers are too at home in the world of the Roman Empire, too involved in cultural practices such as idolatry and eating food offered to idols (2:14). They need to live distinctive and faithful lives

4. See Warren Carter, *What Does Revelation Reveal? Unlocking the Mystery* (Nashville: Abingdon, 2011).

because cultural accommodation threatens their witness and discipleship (Rev. 2:1–17). Chapters 4–5 offer a contrasting revelation of true worship as John enters the heavens and witnesses heavenly worship of God as creator (chap. 4) and redeemer (chap. 5). Chapters 6–7 reveal that judgment on the Roman imperial world is taking place now, though the world has a chance to repent (Rev. 8–11). Chapters 12–14 reveal that the devil is the evil power behind the scenes, inspiring worship of the emperor and controlling the imperial economic system. In the absence of any change, though, Revelation reveals that the time of judgment on Rome's eternal empire has arrived (Rev. 15–18). In its place God's good and life-giving reign is established (chaps. 19–22).

Gospels

The Gospels, like Paul's Letters and like documents such as Hebrews and Revelation, address the specific situations and needs of their communities of Jesus-believers. But the Gospels do so in at least two significantly different ways.[5]

First, they use story mode to do their pastoral and theological work. Whereas the letters expect their audiences to follow the multiple steps of an argument, the Gospels tell a story. While Paul's Letters put forth propositions, the Gospels weave a narrative. Whereas Paul would say "grace," Matthew tells a story of Mary's conception of Jesus by the Holy Spirit, a story of God's gracious initiative (1:18–25). As audiences move forward through the narrative—linking scenes to construct the plot, building characters, evaluating points of view—they learn to be disciples of Jesus. They discern God's point of view and the requisite practices for a faithful way of life.

And second, the Gospels differ from the letters in their presentations of Jesus. Whereas the letters concentrate on Jesus's death, resurrection, and return, the Gospel narratives pay much attention to Jesus's public activity throughout his whole life. The Gospels see God's transforming work as taking place not only in the cross, resurrection, and return, but also across the whole of Jesus's life and activity of teaching, healing, exorcisms, and meals. So in Matthew's Gospel, Jesus is commissioned to manifest God's saving presence at conception (1:21–23). This commission frames the whole of his ministry. There is no "Dear Reader" note that says, "Wait till we get to the cross; everything else doesn't matter." For Matthew's Gospel, all of Jesus's activity matters a great deal. All of it manifests God's saving presence.

5. On the Gospels, see Warren Carter, *Matthew: Storyteller, Interpreter, Evangelist* (Peabody, MA: Hendrickson, 2004); idem, *John: Storyteller, Interpreter, Evangelist* (Peabody, MA: Hendrickson, 2006).

DATING THE GOSPELS

Note these references to the fall of Jerusalem that are located in Jesus's ministry even though they refer to a later time and set of circumstances:

- Matthew 22:1–10 and Luke 14:15–24. Matthew's version of the parable of the great feast turns the meal into a wedding banquet for the king's son. The invitations are refused, and the king is angry (22:7). At this point in Luke's version (14:21), the owner sends slaves to invite the street people. In Matthew's version the king "destroyed those murderers, and burned their city," before hosting the banquet in the smoking ruins. Most interpreters see verse 7 as Matthew's addition (not in Luke) that interprets Rome's burning of Jerusalem in 70 CE as punishment on the city's leaders for rejecting Jesus the Son.

- Mark 13:2. "Do you see these great buildings? Not one stone will be left here upon another; all will be thrown down."

- Luke 19:41–43. Concerning Jerusalem, Luke's Jesus says, "Your enemies will set up ramparts around you and surround you, and hem you in on every side. They will crush you to the ground, you and your children, ... because you did not recognize the time of your visitation from God." The last clause provides a theological interpretation for Jerusalem's destruction in 70 CE in relation to the rejection of Jesus.

- Luke 21:20. "When you see Jerusalem surrounded by armies, then know that its desolation has come near."

- John 11:48. "If we let him go on like this, everyone will believe in him, and the Romans will come and destroy both our holy place and our nation." Typical of John's irony, they do not let Jesus continue; they crucify him. But it does not stop the Romans from destroying Jerusalem in 70 CE, an event that must have happened for this verse to expose their error.

It is not that either the letters or the Gospels have a better approach. But they do have different ways of doing theological and pastoral work.

The Gospels—according to Mark, Matthew, Luke, and John—were written late in the first century, some forty to fifty years after Jesus's death. The clearest indication of their dating comes by way of references to and reflection on the destruction of Jerusalem and its temple by the Romans in 70 CE. In addition, beginning early in the second century, early Christian writings cite

Figure 6.3. Images of the fall of Jerusalem from the Arch of Titus (Gunnar Bach Pedersen/Wikimedia Commons)

(unattributed) material that is found in the Gospels. These dates provide a time period between about 70 and about 100 CE for the composition of the Gospels.

This time gap of some fifty or so years between the time of Jesus (crucified ca. 30 CE) and the time of the Gospels (written ca. 70–100 CE) is significant. It highlights, first of all, the type of writings that the Gospels are. They are not eyewitness accounts of Jesus's ministry, written by Jesus's disciples at the end of a hard day's ministry. They do not pretend to offer disinterested and balanced reporting of "just the facts."

Rather, they are "invested" documents. They are written by insiders for insiders. They have an obvious commitment to Jesus. They elaborate his significance for discipleship. So the Gospels begin with confessions:

- "The beginning of the good news of Jesus Christ, the Son of God" (Mark 1:1).
- "An account of the genealogy of Jesus the Messiah, the son of David, the son of Abraham" (Matt. 1:1).
- "In the beginning was the Word" (John 1:1–18).

These confessions are elaborated through the narratives with insights that, through the fifty years since the time of Jesus, have emerged in the church's activities of preaching, teaching, worshiping, practical caring, and reflection on the significance of Jesus. John 12:16 expresses something of this process of insight: "His disciples did not understand these things at first; but when Jesus was glorified, then they remembered that these things had been written of him and had been done to him." The Gospels are postresurrection writings. They are written from the vantage point of the end of the story, looking backward (as also indicated in Mark 9:9–10; John 2:22; 20:9).

Presenting Jesus

Jesus is the main character in the Gospel stories, but the four Gospels do not present him in the same way.

Mark presents him as the agent of God's reign, the one who reveals God's purposes through his activity (1:14–15). Yet Jesus emerges as a paradoxical figure, somewhat mysterious and self-concealing. He is commonly identified as teaching (1:21–22) or as "Teacher" (4:38), but Mark's Gospel does not include much of his teaching, and not many folks seem to learn from

Figure 6.4. Matthew writing his Gospel (Rama/Wikimedia Commons)

him anyway. Disciples follow him, but like the crowds they do not understand him (4:13, 40–41; 8:14–21). A few outsiders—even demons, surprisingly—understand him (1:23–24, 34; 5:7), but he tells them not to tell anyone about him (5:43; 7:36; 8:30). And at the end of the Gospel, Jesus is declared to be risen from the dead, but he does not appear in 16:1–8.[6]

Matthew and Luke present Jesus in a much less mysterious way. Matthew establishes Jesus's mission to manifest God's saving presence from the outset in his conception (1:21–23). This commission interprets all his subsequent actions in his public activity that begins in 4:17. Luke, like Matthew and unlike Mark, leads slowly into Jesus's public activity. Luke's opening chapters place Jesus amid Israel's life in relation to God's faithfulness. Addressing the insecurity or uncertainty of some believers, the Gospel wants believers like Theophilus to know "security" or "certainty" about God's purposes being worked out in Jesus (Luke 1:4 my trans.). Jesus's activity as God's Son or agent in the line of David is to embody God's reign (1:32–33). Jesus begins his public ministry at Nazareth on a Sabbath by applying the words of Isaiah 61 to himself (Luke

---

6. A longer version of the Gospel's ending (16:9–20) was added sometime later in the second or third centuries.

4:18–21). God's Spirit has anointed or commissioned him to "bring good news to the poor, . . . proclaim release to the captives and recovery of sight to the blind, to let the oppressed go free, to proclaim the year of the Lord's favor" (Luke 4:18). This tradition of social release and divine favor frames his public activity as he journeys from Galilee to Jerusalem (chaps. 9–19), to death and resurrection (chaps. 19–24).

John's Gospel presents Jesus as the revealer of God's life-giving purposes. He comes from God: he comes down from heaven (6:38) to reveal what he has seen God do (5:19) and heard God say (14:10, 24). By receiving and entrusting themselves to this revelation, people come to know God (1:12; 17:3) and enter into "eternal life" (3:16; 5:24). This life participates in the partial completion of God's purposes, which Jesus has been revealing in his works of abundant fertility and wholeness (2:1–11; 4:46–54; 6:1–14).

Becoming Disciples

The purpose of these Gospel accounts is not simply to give information about Jesus. Rather, their pastoral-theological purpose is to strengthen understanding of and commitment to Jesus, thereby shaping the identity and way of life of Jesus-followers. In addition to their presentations of Jesus, the Gospels do this disciple-forming work in various ways.

Mark's fast-paced story initially portrays the disciples as characters who are called to be with Jesus, to proclaim, and to have power (3:13–15). They are supposed to understand Jesus (4:10–12), but consistently they don't have a clue. Jesus challenges them to choose faith rather than fear, to know understanding rather than incomprehension (4:40–41; 8:14–21). But when Jesus is crucified, the male disciples run away (14:50). At Jesus's tomb, a heavenly being instructs some women disciples to tell the male disciples to meet the risen Jesus in Galilee. The women, though, "said nothing to anyone, for they were afraid" (16:6–8). This sudden ending confronts the Gospel's audience with a choice between faithful living and fearful silence.

Matthew employs another technique. In his Gospel he includes five big blocks of teaching material in which Jesus explicitly and directly instructs disciples about their identity and way of life. In chapters 5–7, right after the calling of the first disciples in 4:18–22, comes the Sermon on the Mount, which delineates the life of discipleship. In Matthew 10, Jesus teaches about a life of mission, in chapter 13 about a life shaped by God's reign, and in chapter 18 about the communal dimensions of discipleship. Chapters 24–25 outline the eschatological completion of God's purposes; disciples are to live now in accord with those purposes.

Luke presents discipleship as imitating Jesus by adding a sequel to the Gospel. The book of Acts is part 2 of a two-part work, even though they are separated in the canon by John's Gospel. Acts focuses on the activity of Jesus's followers. The distinctive thing about their activity is that they imitate Jesus. So Jesus is empowered by the Spirit (Luke 4:18), as are his followers at Pentecost (Acts 2). Jesus teaches about his death and resurrection (Luke 9:22; 18:31–33; 24:44–46), as do his followers (Acts 4:10–12; 17:3). Jesus casts out demons, heals the sick, and raises the dead (Luke 4:31–37; 5:17–26; 7:11–17), as do his followers (Acts 19:12; 20:7–12). Jesus requires the sharing of property and wealth (Luke 6:35), which his followers do (Acts 4:32–34). Discipleship is about imitating Jesus.

Figure 6.5. Luke writing his Gospel (Kevin Wailes/Wikimedia Commons)

John's Gospel emphasizes the role of Jesus-followers in continuing Jesus's ministry. Through the first twelve chapters, they witness the revelation of God's life-giving purposes in Jesus's ministry. Then, in chapters 13–17, Jesus has a retreat with the disciples. He instructs them on how they are to live in his absence as he returns to God (13:1). He emphasizes their love for one another (13:33–34), their doing even "greater works" than Jesus (14:12), the presence of the Paraclete or Spirit with them to guide them (14:15–16, 25–26), their following Jesus's teaching (14:21), their drawing life from the risen Jesus (15:1–11), and their encountering opposition from a society that lives by different values and practices (15:18–25).

Figure 6.6. Image of John (Theodoros/ Wikimedia Commons)

Synoptic Gospels

In these diverse presentations, the Gospel writers are working with traditions about Jesus to interpret his significance for discipleship. Readers have long noticed that John's Gospel is significantly different from the other three: Mark, Matthew, and Luke. These three often seem to be similar, though they also have some significant differences. They include many of the same stories, sometimes with identical wording, and sometimes in the same order. Because of this look-alike quality, they are called "Synoptic" Gospels. The word "Synoptic" combines two words, "together" (*syn*) and "seeing" (*optic*). How, then, did these three Gospels come to be both similar and yet different? This question is known as the "Synoptic Problem": how to account for the similarities and differences among these three Gospels.

The most common explanation recognizes three factors: the roles of sources or traditions about Jesus, the crucial role of the Gospel authors, and the significance of the situations that the Gospels address.

The levels of similarity suggest some common written sources and literary interdependence among the three Gospels, at least in places. The common view is that Mark's Gospel was the first to be written, and that both Matthew and Luke use Mark as a source. Matthew, for example, includes all but about 55 verses of Mark's approximate 660 verses. Matthew and Luke do not simply take over Mark; they edit or redact Mark in order to express distinct theological understandings and to address the particular circumstances of their audiences. For example, we noticed above that while Mark regularly refers to Jesus teaching, Mark's Gospel does not include extensive accounts of *what* Jesus taught. Matthew rectifies this lack by expanding two of Mark's main collections (cf. Mark 4 and Matt. 13; Mark 13 and Matt. 24–25) and by inserting three blocks of teaching material where Mark has none (Matt. 5–7; 10; 18). Matthew 5–7 composes the Sermon on the Mount. Its insertion into Mark's narrative can be seen very clearly by comparing Mark 1:16–20 with Matthew 4:18–22; Mark 1:21 with Matthew 4:23–25; 5:1–2; and Mark 1:22 with Matthew 7:28–29.

While Matthew and Luke draw on Mark, both Matthew (chap. 28) and Luke (chap. 24) are much longer than Mark (chap. 16). Where does the extra material come from? About a quarter of both Matthew and Luke consists of material common to these two Gospels but absent from Mark. Often this material is similar in wording and order. Some have explained these similarities by proposing a second literary source that only the authors of Matthew and Luke used. This source (referred to as Q, from the German word *Quelle* meaning "source," and not from a James Bond movie) has never been discovered, but it has been plausibly reconstructed. Theoretically, it comprises sayings attributed

MATTHEW EDITING OR REDACTING MARK

Matthew redacts or edits Mark's story of Jesus's calming the sea (Mark 4:35–41). In Matthew 8:23–27, Matthew turns a story that celebrates Jesus's power over nature into a story about the danger yet power of discipleship. Notice these changes:

- Matthew relocates the story to a new context, right after a section on discipleship (8:18–22).
- Matthew introduces the story with the key discipleship verb: "his disciples followed him" (8:23).
- In 8:24 Matthew changes Mark's Greek word for the "storm." Matthew uses the same word in 24:7 to denote disruptions and trials as the end of the age approaches. Matthew's new word from this context represents the "storm" as typical of the "storms" or challenges of discipleship.
- In Matthew 8:25 the disciples, in danger on the stormy sea, cry out to Jesus not as "Teacher" as in Mark 4:38, but with the confessional term "Lord." They ask Jesus, "Save us," rather than accusing him with, "Do you not care that we are perishing?" (Mark 4:38).
- In Matthew 8:26 Jesus addresses the disciples as "You of little faith" rather than with Mark's question, "Why are you afraid?" (8:40). Matthew's Jesus recognizes that the disciples have some faith in crying out in a difficult situation. Jesus challenges them to have more faith rather than rebuking them for having none.

These changes heighten discipleship elements in Matthew's account. Although Jesus still performs a miracle, Matthew's retelling reorients the story to show Jesus's powerful response to disciples caught in difficult circumstances.

to Jesus, along with the temptation narrative (Matt. 4:1–11; Luke 4:1–13) and the healing of the centurion's slave/son (Matt. 8:5–13; Luke 7:1–10). Some scholars have argued that it was an oral collection of material rather than a written one.

As with Mark material, Matthew and Luke edit or redact Q sayings to fit their own particular agenda. A good example of this redaction occurs with the parable of the one sheep that is lost from the flock of one hundred sheep. Luke's telling and placement of the parable emphasizes the party that breaks out when the sheep is recovered (Luke 15:3–7). It was lost but now is found. Luke places this parable right after criticism of Jesus's welcoming reception for undesirable tax collectors (who cooperated with the occupying Romans) and "sinners" (a name reserved for anyone you don't like). This placement addresses this criticism by showing a heavenly party for those who as repentant sinners receive Jesus's message.

Matthew gives the same parable a very different spin. First, he includes it in chapter 18. This chapter is not concerned with the criticism of outsiders. Rather, it focuses on how disciples should relate to one another. Matthew edits the introduction and conclusion of the parable (18:10, 14) so that instead of referring to welcoming "sinful" or undesirable outsiders, it instructs Jesus's followers to look after each other and actively care for every one of his disciples (18:15–20).

Matthew and Luke thus expand Mark's basic outline of the story of Jesus by adding material from their common source, Q. They also include additional material that is unique to each of them. Staying with alphabet letters, material unique to Matthew is identified as M, and material unique to Luke is L. Both M and L seem to be fairly loose collections of traditions.

This model of how the Gospels came to be written explains the similarities and differences of each Gospel in terms of three moving parts. One concerns the sources that are shared by Matthew and Luke. The dominant theory—the Two-Document Hypothesis—posits Matthew and Luke as using Mark and Q, with M and L unique to Matthew and Luke respectively. Second, this theory recognizes that each Gospel's author (or authors) uses these sources creatively. They expand, abbreviate, omit, and relocate material. By this redaction, they shape narratives that express their interpretations of the significance of Jesus. And third, they redact or shape these traditions to address the particular situations or circumstances of their communities of Jesus-followers. Their narratives are story sermons, the means by which they do their pastoral work in addressing a word-on-target for the specific circumstances of communities of Jesus-followers.

What, then, are Gospels? From our discussion we might describe them in this way in one long dense sentence: the Gospels shaped and interpreted traditions about Jesus into story form in order to proclaim the significance of Jesus for the identity and way of life of a community of Jesus-disciples in the post–70 CE era.

Conclusion

In the period between ca. 50 and ca. 130 CE, the documents that will later compose the New Testament are written. These documents are diverse in form (the Letters, the Gospels, Hebrews, Revelation) and in their theological understandings. They are all concerned to help communities of Jesus-believers live faithfully to their commitment to him. In the next chapter we think about how these writings become the New Testament.

The Process of "Closing" the New Testament Canon
(397 CE)

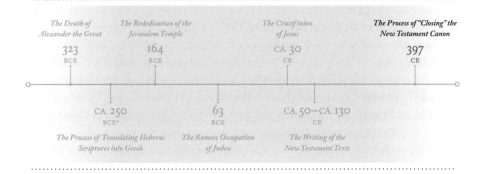

The Death of Alexander the Great	The Rededication of the Jerusalem Temple		The Crucifixion of Jesus	The Process of "Closing" the New Testament Canon
323 BCE	164 BCE		CA. 30 CE	397 CE
	CA. 250 BCE*	63 BCE	CA. 50—CA. 130 CE	
	The Process of Translating Hebrew Scriptures into Greek	The Roman Occupation of Judea	The Writing of the New Testament Texts	

The New Testament is so much a part of the Christian tradition that we think it was always there. Not so. As strange as it sounds, the church existed for several centuries without a New Testament canon. Nor did the New Testament suddenly drop out of the sky, precooked and divinely created. Rather, the New Testament canon came into being through various historical factors and processes during a number of centuries. The church produced the canon.

How did this happen?

Our seventh key event, involving the formation of the New Testament canon, stretches the meaning of the word "event" in several ways. First, this so-called event involves a process that stretched across at least 350 years. As we saw in the last chapter, most of the writings that would later form the New Testament were written between the years ca. 50 CE and ca. 130 CE, but they did not exist as a widely recognized, authoritative collection—as a canon, or "rule"—for several more centuries. One of the key events involved in that recognition of the canon happened at the end of the fourth century. In 397 CE,

133

a regional church council, the Council of Carthage in North Africa, ratified the New Testament canon as the authoritative writings for their churches. This action was not a sudden or surprising event. It belonged to a process in the church's life stretching back over three or so centuries.[1]

Second, this event concerning the canon in 397 CE was significant for some, but not for all, churches at the end of the fourth century. We must be careful not to overstate its importance. It would be inappropriate, for example, to claim that in 397 CE at this meeting in Carthage, the whole church declared the canon officially closed. It would be incorrect to assert that in 397 CE the Council of Carthage culminated all discussion about a canon and settled it for all time for all churches with a decree closing the canon. That would be to claim too much, as we will see. That is why in the title for this chapter I have placed the word "closing" in quotation marks. What we can say is that the declaration at the Council of Carthage in 397 CE was an important marker, for *some* churches, a moment in which *a number of* churches, but not all churches, recognized the canon as closed. For a significant number of churches, the council recognized these twenty-seven writings as authoritative for their practice and doctrine.

So with these qualifications in mind for this chapter, we sketch out five stages in this process toward closing the canon, we nuance the use of the word "closing" in relation to the Council of Carthage's declaration in 397 CE, we identify some of the criteria involved in writings making it into the canon, and we recognize several questions that some people have raised about the significance of the church's having a New Testament canon.

Process of Formation

We begin with three brief observations.

First, in talking of the process that formed the New Testament canon, we have to be careful not to get the cart before the horse. Identifying stages in this

1. Helpful for this chapter have been Werner Georg Kümmel, *Introduction to the New Testament* (London: SCM, 1975), 475–510; Bart Ehrman, *Lost Scriptures: Books That Did Not Make It into the New Testament* (New York: Oxford University Press, 2003); Lee Martin McDonald and James A. Sanders, eds., *The Canon Debate* (Peabody, MA: Hendrickson, 2003); Lee Martin McDonald, *The Biblical Canon: Its Origin, Transmission, and Authority* (Peabody, MA: Hendrickson, 2007); Craig A. Evans and Emanuel Tov, eds., *Exploring the Origins of the Bible: Canon Formation in Historical, Literary, and Theological Perspective* (Grand Rapids: Baker Academic, 2008); Luke Timothy Johnson, *The Writings of the New Testament* (Minneapolis: Fortress, 2010), 525–46; Lee Martin McDonald, *The Origin of the Bible: A Guide for the Perplexed* (London: T&T Clark, 2011).

process can be done only from the end and looking backward, not from the beginning and looking forward. No one in the first century CE was planning the canon. No one had mapped out a timeline with a five-stage process. Paul did not say to himself, after a busy day's writing of Romans: "This is some of my better work; I must send it to the canon selection committee!" There was no such committee. The idea of a canon, or collection of authoritative writings, emerges gradually over centuries, as we shall see. As surprisingly unspiritual as it may seem, much of the process was unofficial and uncoordinated rather than self-conscious and intentional.

Second, parts of the process remain elusive to us. Since there was no committee, there were no secretaries and no minutes. There are gaps in our knowledge. At best, we can see parts of the process, connect some dots, and hypothesize about parts; we remain ignorant of the rest. In identifying five stages, I am not suggesting that these are distinct and separate periods. They overlap and are interconnected.

And third, we saw in chapter 2 that the Septuagint (the translation of the Hebrew Scriptures into Greek: LXX) was the Scripture of the church. Reading with their Jesus-glasses on, they saw and heard references to Jesus that no other readers had seen or heard. That is, parts of the Septuagint tradition functioned as a resource in providing language and ideas to interpret the significance of Jesus. As writings from Jesus-believers came into being, they initially existed in the shadow of the authoritative LXX writings. Only with time did writings from Jesus-believers gain parity.

Stage 1: Writing

In the last chapter, we posited ca. 50 to ca. 130 CE as the likely time period in which the writings that would later form the New Testament collection were written. The window is, of course, approximate. None of the documents was written during the time of Jesus (pre–ca. 30 CE). Seven Letters of Paul are widely regarded to be the earliest writings in the New Testament, originating mostly in the 50s CE (Romans, 1 and 2 Corinthians, Galatians, Philippians, 1 Thessalonians, Philemon), with perhaps 1 Thessalonians or Galatians as the earliest, dating from (late in?) the 40s CE. Beyond these seven Letters, the Gospels are usually dated in the ca. 70–100 CE window, as is Revelation, with some such as Acts, 2 Peter, and 1 Timothy possibly in the 100–130 CE period.

Significantly, as we also observed in chapter 6, these writings that will later form the New Testament emerge from and address believing communities. They are reflective of, rooted in, and turned toward the church's life. It is not

DIVERSE WORSHIP MATERIAL IN THE NEW TESTAMENT

- Philippians 2:6–11 is a hymn; some think Paul edited verse 8 by adding "even death on a cross." Paul includes this hymn not for the purposes of doctrinal instruction, and not for worship purposes, but to exhort Jesus-believers to behave a certain way, seeking the good of the other (2:4–5).
- Traditions about the Lord's Supper are presented in 1 Corinthians 11:17–34, especially 23–24.
- Language from prayers also appears, including Greek-lettered approximations of Amēn, the Hebrew word that confirms or agrees with what is prayed (1 Cor. 14:16; 2 Cor. 1:20; Gal. 1:5; 6:18); the Aramaic cry Maranatha, "Our Lord, come," as an anticipation of Jesus's return (1 Cor. 16:22); and the Aramaic address for God in prayer, "Abba! Father!" (Mark 14:36; Rom. 8:15; Gal. 4:6).
- Confessions are also included, such as existing doctrinal affirmations (1 Cor. 15:3–7) or creedal statements that might have begun with something like "I/we believe in . . ." (Rom. 1:3–4; 4:24b–25).

Beyond Paul, we find hymns cited, as in Colossians 1:15–20 and perhaps in Revelation 5:9–10 and 15:3 (if they are not just literary creations). Either a hymn or a confession is used in 1 Timothy 3:16. The Lord's Prayer appears in two different versions in Matthew 6:9–13 and Luke 11:2–4. Perhaps the two versions reflect the different forms of this prayer used in worship by the believers for whom these Gospels were especially written. Rituals such as baptism (Rom. 6:3–4; Matt. 28:19–20) and the Lord's Supper (Mark 14:22–25; Luke 22:14–23) appear in the Gospels, as does a process for church discipline (Matt. 18:15–20). There are controversy stories, such as those about fasting (Mark 2:18–22) or how to honor the Sabbath (Mark 2:23–28; 3:1–6) or what to eat (Mark 7:18–19; Acts 10:13–16; 15:20). These scenes may reflect disputes between Jesus-followers and other groups, as well as disputes *among* Jesus-followers for whom the scenes provide guidance and instruction. The Letter to the Hebrews reads like a sermon or perhaps a compilation of sermons.

surprising, then, that various writings include material like hymns, confessions, prayers, and rituals used in the worship life of Jesus-believing communities.

It is also clear that these writings emerge out of a context dominated by oral communication. Writing did not stop the oral transmission of traditions. Material continued to circulate in oral form along with written documents.

Much of the tradition about Jesus remained flexible and malleable, shaping oral and written material to address community needs. Even a written Gospel like Mark was edited (redacted) or rewritten at least twice—by both Matthew and Luke. Yet Mark did not get left behind. The dire warning in the book of Revelation against messing with anything is certainly not applicable to the Jesus traditions (Rev. 22:18–19).

The recognition of coexisting oral and written material raises an interesting question: Why was anything written at all, especially in a culture where many were illiterate and orality served many well? We don't know for sure and can only guess at some of the factors that account for the emergence of written documents.

Certainly for Paul, his letters were a surrogate for his presence. Through his letters, he was able to be in several locations at once. They were a means of doing his pastoral ministry. He writes, he says, so that his readers can understand his teaching (2 Cor. 1:13). He writes "rather boldly" to the believers in Rome (Rom. 15:15) before he is able to see them (1:9–15). The letter prepares them for a visit (15:24). Writing communicates his concerns and explains his actions to the Thessalonians (1 Thess. 3:5). Writing ensures geographical access and presence when the writer is absent.

Letters seem to be a particularly good medium for this purpose of addressing particular communities and substituting for absent leaders and teachers. Perhaps that's one of the reasons why most of the New Testament collection comprises letters or at least writings that exhibit features of letters. Twenty of the twenty-seven documents are letters, to which we should cautiously add Hebrews and Revelation. Hebrews does not begin as a letter but addresses its audience directly throughout (2:1; 3:1; 6:1; 10:19; 12:1). It ends in chapter 13 with features of a letter: short commands, a benediction, a reference to Timothy and a possible visit, the sending of greetings, and a closing benediction. In the second century it was identified as "the Letter to the Hebrews." And the book of Revelation, which identifies itself as a "revelation" (or apocalypse) in verse 1 and a "prophecy" in verse 3, employs the letter form in 1:4. It has the common salutation that identifies the sender and the recipients, and then greets them:

> John to the seven churches that are in Asia:
> Grace to you and peace . . .

The whole work is thereby framed as a letter. And in chapters 2–3, it employs letters within the letter, addressing the seven letters to churches in the Roman province of Asia.

Figure 7.1. The great altar of Pergamum, one of the churches addressed in Revelation (Jan Mehlich/Wikimedia Commons)

Two of the Gospels express their purposes in terms similar to those Paul uses to express his purposes. Luke tells Theophilus that he has written so that Theophilus might "know security/certainty/assurance concerning the things about which [he has] received (religious) instruction" (Luke 1:4 my trans.). The Gospel provides pastoral reassurance for a situation of insecurity or uncertainty about God's purposes. In John's Gospel the author says, "These are written that you may come to believe that Jesus is the Messiah, the Son of God, and that through believing you may have life in his name" (John 20:31). Concerning the verb "believe," there is a dispute as to whether it should be translated "come to believe" or "continue to believe." The former option is evangelistic; the latter option (which seems more convincing) is about sustaining discipleship.

In addition to making present someone who is absent, writing codifies and formalizes material. The passing of time stimulates such a need. Toward the end of the first century, people who knew Jesus or were companions of Paul were dying or had died. The second coming of Jesus (called the parousia) had not happened. Practices and understandings among groups of Jesus-followers continued to diversify. Conflicts about identity increased. Gentiles became increasingly dominant in the church. Groups needed structure and leaders. These factors meant that the church had to come to grips with the passing of time, with being around for the long haul, with being permanent members of society. Writing provided a means of articulating the church's identity. Writing carefully and permanently codified acceptable practices and understandings in these developing and diverse circumstances.

Thus 1 Peter exhorts its audience to live faithfully, hopefully, and actively by doing good works in society. Its readers in the widespread provinces of "Pontus, Galatia, Cappadocia, Asia, and Bithynia" (1:1) are to undergo suffering, if necessary, and publicly witness to the good news of God's action in Christ. First John addresses a congregation that has been in conflict and has

EARLY WRITINGS NOT IN THE CANON

Writings from around 100 CE include the following. Most of these have survived.[1]

- In Colossians 4:16 is a confusing reference to a letter "from Laodicea." It is not clear whether this letter comes from the church in Laodicea or from the same person writing Colossians in Paul's name. This letter has not survived, though sometime in the second century someone tried to fill in the gap and wrote such a letter.

- *First Clement* was written perhaps in the 90s (though it is uncertain). This letter comes from a leader in the church at Rome to the Corinthians after some in Corinth rebelled against certain leaders and divisions resulted. It survives.

- The very passionate Ignatius, who wrote seven letters, was leader of the church in Antioch, Syria; sometime around 100–110 he was arrested and taken to Rome. Along the way he writes from Smyrna to four churches (*To the Romans*, *To the Ephesians*, *To the Magnesians*, *To the Trallians*); then from Troas he writes three more letters (*To the Philadelphians*, *To the Smyrnaeans*, and *To Polycarp*, the leader of the congregation in Smyrna). Ignatius thanks the churches for support, addresses the problem of division, and focuses on the death of Jesus. These letters have survived.

- The title of the *Didache* is the Greek word for "Teaching." This document has survived and comprises a church manual written for church leaders. It offers a wonderful glimpse into church life, perhaps as early as the 70s CE. The first part provides moral instruction about how to live and how not to live (the two ways). The second part gives instructions for ordering congregational life, including baptism, fasting, prayer, the Eucharist, recognizing itinerant teachers and apostles and prophets, worship, and local leaders (bishops and deacons).

- *Gospel of Thomas*: Copies of this book have survived, presenting 114 sayings attributed to Jesus: about half of them bear some resemblance to the Synoptic Gospels, and others are quite different. Scholars debate when the collection was made, with suggestions from the late first century through the third century. There are several other gospels (*Gospel of the Nazoreans*, *Gospel of the Ebionites*, *Gospel according to the Hebrews*) whose dates of origin are unclear, but they may have originated early in the second century.

[1] Texts can be found online or in Bart Ehrman, *Lost Scriptures: Books That Did Not Make It into the New Testament* (New York: Oxford University Press, 2003).

split. Some, whom the author labels negatively as "antichrists" in 2:18–19, either departed voluntarily or were expelled. The letter makes sense of this event by pointing out the errors of these renegades' thinking about Christ (4:2) and moral living (3:4–8; 2:9–11). It reasserts "proper" understanding and practices, at least as the author interprets them. First Timothy is also concerned with diverse thinking and practices. It circles the wagons by establishing recognized leaders called bishops and deacons as a way to provide boundaries and authority (3:1–13).

All the documents that would later become part of the New Testament collection were written in the time period of ca. 50–ca. 130. But not everything written in this time period ends up in the New Testament. In the last chapter we noticed that our 1 and 2 Corinthians refer to two other letters that did not survive. It's not hard to imagine that the Corinthians did not highly value a letter that Paul himself describes as written "out of much distress and anguish of heart and with many tears" (2 Cor. 2:4). It was probably not one of their communal keepsakes! We also noted a possible document called Q, which may have existed in written form in perhaps the 50s CE. This was a possible collection of sayings of Jesus that Matthew and Luke (not Mark) purportedly used to expand Mark's Gospel. It did not survive. Other documents existing in about 100 CE include Ignatius's letters, *1 Clement*, and the *Didache*, but they did not make it into the New Testament canon.

Stage 2: Use

The second stage in the process of the formation of the New Testament canon involves the use or reading/hearing of these texts among Jesus-believing communities. The writings, of course, were not private communications for individuals: they addressed communities. Even the Letter to Philemon is addressed to "Apphia our sister, . . . Archippus, . . . and to the church in your house." The writings were read aloud in the assemblies. Colossians 4:16 mentions its own reading: "And when this letter has been read among you . . ." The writer of Revelation declares, "Blessed is the one who reads aloud the words of the prophecy, and blessed are those who hear" (1:3).

Writings came to be read not just in the church to which they were addressed, but also in various churches. Second Corinthians is addressed to the church "in Corinth" but also to "all the saints [believers] throughout Achaia" (2 Cor. 1:1). Achaia was the Roman province covering southern Greece, including the cities of Athens and Sparta in addition to Corinth. The greeting invites its reading in centers beyond the city of Corinth. Acts 15:23 reports a "regional letter" being sent to the churches of Antioch, Syria, and Cilicia, a missive that has not survived.

First Peter addresses believers across a widespread area in the provinces of "Pontus, Galatia, Cappadocia, Asia, and Bithynia" (1:1). Revelation addresses seven cities individually in letters (Rev. 2–3), but assumes that the whole document (part letter, prophecy, and apocalypse) will be read in each place. The Colossians are instructed to make sure their letter is read to the Laodicean believers and that the Colossians read the letter to/from Laodicea (4:16).

Through the second century, Gospels written originally for particular communities are being read in various assemblies across a wider geographical area. We get some idea of this practice from Justin, who, writing in the middle of the second century in Rome, offers a general description of worship:

> And on the day called Sunday, all who live in cities or in the country gather together in one place, *and the memoirs of the apostles or the writings of the prophets are read*, as long as time permits; then, when the reader has ceased, the Ruler in a discourse instructs and exhorts to the imitation of these good things. Then we all stand up together and offer prayers; and, as we before said, when we have finished the prayer, bread is brought and wine and water, and the ruler likewise offers up prayers and thanksgivings, to the best of his ability, and the people assent, saying the Amen; and the distribution and the partaking of the eucharistized elements is to each. . . . And they who prosper, and so wish, contribute what each thinks fit; and what is collected is deposited with the Ruler, who takes care of the orphans and widows, and those who, on account of sickness or any other cause, are in want.
>
> Justin, *First Apology* 67[2]

Several things about the Gospels are evident in Justin's very interesting account of worship in the mid-second century CE. He uses a plural term to refer to the Gospels as "memoirs of the apostles," but does not specify which ones he has in mind. We can deduce from all his writings that he knows Matthew, Mark, and Luke, but he does not seem to know John. Second, he indicates that readings from these memoirs take place along with the Prophets from the LXX. He does not indicate whether the memoirs are treated with parity. Third, how much weight these readings have is not clear. Such readings, he says, happen only "as time permits." They do not seem to be an absolutely fixed practice. Fourth, while Justin generalizes his description—"This is what *we* do"—it is not clear how widespread in churches were the practices he describes.

Three important issues emerge from the use of these writings. As they are read in different places, the issue of relevance comes to the fore. Writings

---

2. Leslie William Barnard, trans., *St. Justin Martyr: The First and Second Apologies*, Ancient Christian Writers 56 (New York: Paulist Press, 1997), 71, emphasis added.

written originally to a particular situation are heard in very different situations. Could they speak to other contexts and become generally relevant writings? Second, as writings become used in worship, the question of their status in relation to the authoritative LXX writings arises. Initially they clearly do not have the same status. But through the second and third centuries, this changes.[3] And third, the sharing of writings among various communities of Jesus-believers creates a sense of various local groups belonging to a larger movement.

Stage 3: Collections

As writings came to be used in assemblies, and as copies were made and circulated, collections of writings inevitably developed. The emergence of collections is a sign that writings were passing the relevance test and were useful beyond the immediate context for which they had been written. Three sets of collections emerge that are important for the formation of the New Testament canon: Paul's Letters, the four Gospels, and the so-called General Epistles. What we know as the canon is, in fact, a collection of these three collections.

We can trace out something of the move toward the collection of the four Gospels. By around 100 CE, Gospels were circulating. Luke mentions previous accounts of Jesus's activity without specifying that Mark and perhaps Q are at least two of these (Luke 1:1–4). Ignatius (ca. 110) seems to know Matthew and John (without saying so specifically). Justin in the mid-second century refers to the "memoirs of the apostles" without mentioning specific Gospels. He probably means Matthew, Mark, and Luke.

Some in the second century found the existence of multiple and different Gospels problematic. In about 180 or so, Tatian addresses this issue by conflating the four gospels, plus some other material, into one version called the *Diatessaron* (from Greek words meaning "through/with four"). Tatian creates his own narrative sequence from the four Gospels and removes contradictory material like the genealogies. The *Diatessaron* was widely used in Syrian churches for several centuries. While Tatian collects the four Gospels into one document, he clearly does not think their texts are fixed and inviolable. Nor does he think that having four separate Gospels is a good idea; he wants just one harmonized version. The fact that the *Diatessaron* was not widely adopted beyond the Syrian churches indicates a conscious embracing of the diverse and multiple accounts of Jesus's activity

3. McDonald (*Origin of the Bible*, 135–47) traces out some of this process.

and significance. This affirmation will be expressed in the choice of the four Gospels for the canon.

Around the same time (180 CE), Irenaeus, bishop of Lyons in South France, argues that there should be an exclusive collection of *four* Gospels. He condemns those who use only one Gospel—Ebionites (Matthew), Marcion (Luke), and the gnostic Valentinus (John)—along with those who use more than Irenaeus's four (*Haer.* 3.11.7–9). Why should there be four? Irenaeus (imaginatively) argues that "since there are four zones of the world in which we live, and four principal winds [presumably north, south, east, and west], while the church is scattered throughout all the world," it is only right that there should be four Gospels (*Haer.* 3.11.8).[4] The fact that Irenaeus has to argue for a collection of four Gospels indicates that this was not a widely accepted idea yet in the late second century.

By the first half of the third century, however, there is evidence for a collection of the four Gospels. A manuscript called the Chester Beatty papyrus ($\mathfrak{P}^{45}$) provides the earliest evidence for the collection of the four separate Gospels (plus Acts).

The second emerging collection of material involves Paul's Letters. By the early second century, references in Ignatius (*Eph.* 12.2, "in every Epistle") and 2 Peter (3:15–16, "in all his letters") indicate that they knew at least several of Paul's Letters in circulation. Around 140 CE, Marcion provides the first evidence for a collection of letters associated with Paul. He lists (in his order) Galatians, 1 and 2 Corinthians, Romans, 1 and 2 Thessalonians, Ephesians (which he calls Laodiceans), Colossians, Philippians, and Philemon. He does not include 1–2 Timothy and Titus. A manuscript from about 200 CE (Chester Beatty $\mathfrak{P}^{46}$) attests a collection of eleven letters, though with some different entries and in a different order from longest to shortest: Romans, Hebrews, 1 and 2 Corinthians, Ephesians, Galatians, Philippians, Colossians, 1 and 2 Thessalonians, Philemon. The inclusion of Hebrews shows that some thought it was written by Paul (it wasn't). Just who was responsible for these collections, whether key individuals or a Pauline school, is not clear. These collections show, though, that the Letters had passed the relevance test (the particular becomes general) and had some authority in some congregations.

The third smaller collection concerns the remaining seven letters (James, 1 and 2 Peter, 1–3 John, Jude). These letters were known as the General, or Catholic (in the sense of "universal"), Epistles. While 1 Peter and 1 John had

4. *Ante-Nicene Fathers*, ed. Alexander Roberts and James Donaldson, 10 vols. (Grand Rapids: Eerdmans, 1950–51), 1:428.

some profile in the second and third centuries, this collection was much slower to develop. In contrast to the Letters of Paul and the four Gospels, there is no evidence for an emerging collection of these General Letters in the second and third centuries. It is the fourth-century writer Eusebius who first refers to this collection as Catholic Epistles (*Hist. eccl.* 2.23.25). Eusebius, the bishop of Caesarea, who died in about 340 CE, expresses doubts about the authorship of James and Jude but says that these writings "have been used publicly . . . in most churches" (*Hist. eccl.* 2.23.25).[5]

We have identified three emerging collections of writings: the Gospels, Paul's Letters, the General Epistles. These collections will later form the collection of writings that we know as the New Testament canon. We have focused on these three collections because they were the winners, a focus determined by looking backward from the end of the canon-forming process. In doing so, we run the risk of simplifying a complex and messy situation, and of suggesting that the final selection was inevitable from the beginning. Both impressions are incorrect: it was not simple or inevitable. At the very same time these three collections were emerging, there were lots of other Christian writings in use among believing congregations. Writings such as 1 *Clement*, the *Epistle of Barnabas*, the *Didache*, and the *Shepherd of Hermas* were widely used and highly valued—even though they did not become part of the canon.[6]

Stage 4: Lists and Selection

The process of collecting writings into these three emerging collections is simultaneously a selection process. In collecting certain writings together, churches were indicating which writings they found relevant and helpful. Another sign of this selection process is found in the drawing up of lists of acceptable and unacceptable writings.

One major list is called the Muratorian Canon. There is much debate about the date of this list. Conventionally it has been understood to originate in the late second century, in about 180 CE. Others have argued that it comes from the mid-fourth century and attests a later stage in the process, from about 350 CE. Whenever it was written, it sets out someone's (or some group's) list of important writings as well as other writings strongly disliked by the author(s).[7]

---

5. *Eusebius: The Ecclesiastical History*, trans. Kirsopp Lake and J. E. L. Oulton, 2 vols., Loeb Classical Library (Cambridge: Harvard University Press, 1926–32).

6. Texts can be found online or in Ehrman, *Lost Scriptures*.

7. Text in Ehrman, *Lost Scriptures*, 331–33.

MARCION, MONTANISTS, GNOSTICS
AND THE CANON PROCESS?

Who was Marcion? He was active among the churches in Rome but eventually expelled. He rejected the Hebrew Scriptures because, so he argued, they were concerned with law and not love. He argued that the God of the law was fickle and cruel and thus was not the God of Jesus Christ. Paul alone understood this contrast of law and grace, according to Marcion. Ironically, he saw a radical discontinuity between Israel and the church, contrary to Paul in Romans 11. For Marcion, only ten Letters of Paul (excluding the Pastorals) and an edited version of Luke's Gospel could be authoritative writings. He gathered a number of followers (Marcionites), who established communities across the Roman Empire in the second and third centuries. In terms of the process of the canon's formation, Marcion's emphasis on Paul perhaps added to the growing awareness of authoritative writings, but overall his influence seems quite limited.

Who was Montanus? He was the leader of the Montanists, who emerged in the late second century. Montanus was a prophet who emphasized the experience of the Spirit. His followers were prophets and prophetesses experiencing a fresh outpouring of the Spirit. The movement expected the end of the world. What influence did Montanists have on the formation of the canon? Certainly they emphasized new revelations and the continuing inspiration of the Holy Spirit through exercise of prophecy in the present life of their churches. But they did not seem to be interested in determining authoritative writings. Their presence, though, did highlight the question of the place or locus of revelation. The canon-forming process was looking to the past for revelatory writings, whereas Montanists looked to their present experience.

Who were gnostics? Irenaeus attacks two key theologians and leaders of gnosticism called Valentinus and Basilides. Gnosticism was a diverse movement involving a lower creator god, or demiurge, and a supreme divine being. Gnostics (whose name comes from the Greek word for "knowledge") believed that special knowledge was revealed through a teacher or tradition. The knowledge concerned, among other things, a divine spark that resided in some people and could be set free from the evil material world and return to the supreme divine being. Elements from the Christian movement were mixed with this understanding of the world, human beings, redemption, and God.

What influence did gnostics have on the process of forming the canon? Some have argued that the gnostic concern with secret writings was important in posing the question of authoritative writings and apostolic connections. Gnostics probably contributed to this emerging question, but one of their main opponents, Irenaeus, emphasized more a "rule of faith" by which writings were to be interpreted.

- The list includes twenty-two of the twenty-seven writings that will end up in the New Testament.
- Missing are Hebrews, James, 1 and 2 Peter, and 3 John. These last four writings belong to the General Epistles. The list does not oppose these writings; it simply does not include them.
- It strongly opposes two letters, one to the Laodiceans (remember Col. 4:16) and one to the Alexandrians. It declares that these were "forged in Paul's name . . . [by Marcion], [and] cannot be received into the catholic church."
- It includes the Wisdom of Solomon, which is not a Christian text but is included in Bibles of today in the Apocrypha.
- Along with Revelation, the list includes another writing called the "Revelation or Apocalypse of Peter." It recognizes, though, that "some of us are not willing that the latter be read in church."
- It includes the *Shepherd of Hermas*, which "ought to be read" but "not publicly to the people in church. . . ." What can or can't be read *in church* is clearly an important criterion here, though it is not clear why the *Shepherd of Hermas* cannot be read in church or why it should be read privately.
- It rejects any writings associated with particular gnostic and Montanist figures such as Valentinus (a gnostic), Miltiades (a Montanist and Marcionite?), Basilides (another gnostic), and Montanus.

The Muratorian list works with three categories of writings: the definitely acceptable twenty-two, those not ever to be touched, and others useful for devotional reading in private but not in church.

By about 300 CE, Eusebius provides another snapshot of acceptable and unacceptable writings (*Hist. eccl.* 3.25.1–7). His list has four categories.[8]

- Widely acknowledged writings comprise the four Gospels and Acts, Letters by Paul (fourteen, counting Hebrews, though some dispute Pauline authorship; see 3.3.5–7), 1 John, 1 Peter, and Revelation.
- Disputed writings comprise James, Jude, 2 Peter, 2 and 3 John (Eusebius is not sure who wrote these).
- Some writings have had church use, but he now judges them to be spurious or rejected, including *Shepherd of Hermas, Apocalypse of Peter, Epistle of Barnabas, Didache*, and, for some, Revelation.

8. For text see Ehrman, *Lost Scriptures*, 337–38.

- Some writings, he declares, are "spurious . . . wicked and impious," including gospels in the names of Peter and of Thomas, as well as Acts in the names of Andrew and John.

Eusebius's list is interesting. If we combine categories 1 and 2, we have the twenty-seven writings that will form the New Testament, though Eusebius recognizes that there is dispute about five of these. He also indicates that while he accepts Revelation, others do not. The stock of the writings in category three has fallen considerably, at least in the eyes of some. These were widely used writings in the second and third centuries.

Through the fourth century, momentum toward closing the canon increases. The emperor Constantine took up patronage of the church in the second decade of the fourth century. He exerted pressure to unify and consolidate the church. Theological controversies such as the dispute with Arius increased the pressures to clarify authoritative texts and their interpretation. And through the third and fourth centuries, the increased use of the codex, or book format, in place of the scroll required decisions on which writings were to be included. These pressures are reflected, for example, in a list issued by a council that met in Laodicea in 363 CE. The list from this regional council included most of the writings that would end up in the New Testament, with the exception of Revelation (interestingly, Revelation had addressed the church in Laodicea with a negative letter). It also attributed Hebrews to Paul, even though Hebrews does not identify an author.

On January 7, 367 CE, the bishop of Alexandria, Athanasius (his name means "Immortal," or "Not-Death," an interesting name for a bishop), offers a further very influential list. In his Easter letter of 367 (*Festal Letter 39*), he set out for the first time *in one list* the canon of twenty-seven (and only these) books of the New Testament as authoritative for churches.[9] These writings proclaim a teaching of godliness. No one is to add to or subtract from any of these writings.

He goes on to mention, though, other writings that instruct in "the word piety": Wisdom of Solomon, Wisdom of Sirach, Additions to Esther, Judith, and Tobit, all of which are in the Apocrypha in Bibles of today. In addition, he mentions the *Didache* and the *Shepherd of Hermas*. These seven writings are useful for instruction, but he is clear that they do not have the same authority as the twenty-seven. They are not in his canon. He ends with a general dismissal of unspecified "apocryphal [or secret] books created by heretics." Athanasius dismisses these writings because their authors try to pass them off as ancient books when they are not.

9. For text see Ehrman, *Lost Scriptures*, 339–40.

Figure 7.2. Manuscript Codex Vaticanus, containing the end of Luke and the beginning of John; fourth century (CSNTM.org)

Stage 5: Ratification

The term "ratification" might be misleading if we understand it to mean that Athanasius made a proposal in his letter of 367 CE and that the whole, worldwide church got together to say it was a good idea by formally adopting the canon of twenty-seven writings. This did not happen. There was no formal adoption of the canon at a worldwide or ecumenical council.

Nor was there instant or worldwide approval. Athanasius's list of authoritative writings did not receive immediate and universal agreement. In Alexandria, for example, one of Athanasius's own people, Didymus the Blind, had a different list. It is not clear what Didymus thought of Philemon and 2–3 John, but he definitely included in his canon list the *Shepherd of Hermas*, *Barnabas*, *Didache*, and *1 Clement*.[10] A fourth- or fifth-century manuscript of New Testament writings called Codex Vaticanus omits 1–2 Timothy, Titus, and Revelation. Another manuscript from about the same time, called Codex Sinaiticus, includes the twenty-seven writings, as well as the *Epistle of Barnabas* and the *Shepherd of Hermas*. A list from Cassiodorus (in the 550s in Rome) omits 2 Peter, 2–3 John, Jude, and Hebrews. It seems that Athanasius's list is more prescriptive than it is descriptive, more his hope for what should be happening in churches than a carefully researched report on actual practices.

Clearly there were ongoing discussions and diverse practice. Yet despite this ongoing process, many churches agreed with Athanasius's list and adopted it for their own practice. In 397 CE the regional Council of Carthage in North Africa ratified it as normative practice, declaring that no other writings apart from these twenty-seven canonical writings were to be read in churches as

10. Bart Ehrman, "The New Testament Canon of Didymus the Blind," *Vigiliae Christianae* 37 (1983): 1–21.

"divine Scriptures."[11] As a regional council hoping to gain more support, the Council of Carthage looked to the church in Rome to agree with its ratification, thus expanding a network of churches in agreement over this practice.

With Athanasius's declaration in 367 CE and its ratification by the Council of Carthage in 397 CE, the list of twenty-seven writings comes to be recognized as the canon for many, though not all, churches. This recognition of the twenty-seven writings increasingly gained support. It would be the accepted dominant position of the churches for the next thousand years, though it certainly did not end all debate about the canon for all time. In the sixteenth century, for example, the reformer Martin Luther removed Hebrews, James, Jude, and Revelation from the "proper books." The twenty-seven writings, though, were reaffirmed by the Council of Trent (1546), the Articles of the Church of England (1562, 1571), and the opening chapter of the Reformed movement's Westminster Confession (1647).

Criteria for Canonization

I have sketched out a five-stage process of the formation of the New Testament, beginning with the writing of the documents that would eventually be included, their use in churches, the emergence of collections of material, lists that selected and rejected writings, and (partial) ratification in 397 CE. What factors operated in this process?[12] By what criteria were some writings accepted and some rejected?

For several reasons this is a difficult question to answer. We lack information about parts of the process. We also need to remember that much of the five-stage process sketched above was never well coordinated or official. Accordingly, there was no official list of criteria that everyone used. The operative criteria seem to have been employed inconsistently and randomly. Criteria that might explain why some writings were acceptable seem also to be in play for other writings that were rejected. For example, widespread use in churches was important, but some documents that were widely used (the *Shepherd of Hermas*, *Didache*) did not make it. Links with the name of an apostle were important for some documents, but some writings bearing the names of leading apostles were rejected. Certainly criteria interacted with one another to form checks and balances.

Among important criteria are:

11. For text see Ehrman, *Lost Scriptures*, 341–42.
12. See the discussion in McDonald, *Biblical Canon*, 401–21.

- *Antiquity*: An origin close to the time of Jesus and the apostles was important. This was an important criterion in rejecting "secret" writings or writings that suddenly appeared in the second and third centuries in the name of an apostle. Yet we must also recognize that some "early" writings (if that is what they are), such as the *Gospel of Thomas* (or some form of it) or the *Didache* or Q, were not accepted.

- *Apostolicity*: A link with an apostolic figure who was close to Jesus was important. But such a link did not mean automatic acceptance. There were many documents claiming such a link, so the link needed to be credible. A recognized or traceable line of transmission (apostolic succession) helped to establish credibility.[13] So too did the content of the work.

- *Acceptable theological content*: Writings from Jesus-believers offered much diverse content. There was no single orthodox position from the beginning by which everything else could be judged as heresy. If there had been, the process of canonization would have been very neat and quickly settled. Rather, amid much diversity, by the end of the second century a sense of an acceptable "rule of faith," or *regula fidei*, was emerging for some, especially among a significant group of Jesus-believers who wanted a more unified identity for themselves. Determining the content of this rule of faith is more difficult. It included affirmations about Jesus's humanity, the importance of God's action in Jesus's life and death and resurrection, and the significance of the church and the apostles. Documents that claimed to be written by apostles but did not conform theologically to this rule increasingly came to be rejected.

- *Widespread church use* (catholicity): This criterion embraces geographical and temporal dimensions. Writings needed to be well known by churches across the empire, and especially needed the approval of influential churches (and their leaders) such as Alexandria, Antioch, Ephesus, and Rome. They also needed to have been used in the church's life and liturgy for a long time (antiquity). That is, they needed to be relevant, able to address changing circumstances across a wide cross section of churches. This criterion of use in liturgy and teaching serves as a check against newer documents claiming apostolic origin. Basic to this criterion of widespread use was the issue of relevance: Did churches across an extensive period of time and space, in diverse circumstances, hear the word of God through a particular writing when they gathered for worship?

13. Many scholars today do not think many of the New Testament documents were written by apostles, and so this criterion would not be convincing by current understandings.

The Legacy of the Canon

The word "canon" means a "rule" or a "norm." What sort of "rule" or "norm" did this collection provide for early churches and for the contemporary church? These are complicated questions that have been widely debated. I make two brief observations and raise some questions about a third in closing this chapter.

First, the ratification or closing of the canon put in place boundaries for the emerging Christian tradition and churches. It established the identity of Jesus-believers (or identities; see the next paragraph) within certain limits. How to articulate these limits has been much discussed. Often the limits have been defined in terms of theological claims or especially christological claims, but clearly much more is involved. At a minimum, the limits involve historical continuity, theological focus, institutional structures, and moral practices. Historical continuity was secured through an apostolic connection (or claimed connection) to the time of Jesus, as well as by important connections with Jewish traditions. The theological focus concerned claims about the manifestation of God in Jesus. Institutional structures defined leadership roles, elaborated household and gender roles, and secured practices such as baptism and the Lord's Supper. Moral practices elaborated ways of life and relational interactions consistent with the activity of Jesus and the presence of the Spirit.

Second, within such limits, the canon also legitimized diversity or plurality. Tatian's *Diatessaron*, an attempt to produce just one Gospel account from multiple accounts, was rejected in favor of four Gospels that did not present Jesus in the same way. Marcion's insistence on "Paul alone" was rejected by including Paul's Letters along with the Gospels and the General Epistles. Writings that recognized a communal-relational church structure (Matt. 18) existed alongside a charismatic structure (1 Cor. 12–14) and a hierarchical, office-based structure (1 Timothy). Writings with heavy theological emphases coexisted with writings such as James that had minimal Christology but maximum praxis.

Such diversity or plurality creates both a challenge and an opportunity for believing communities. How does one negotiate this situation? The common saying that you can find a verse in the Bible to support any viewpoint is not quite true, but it does accurately recognize multiple perspectives. As an example, on the one hand, 1 Timothy forbids women to exercise ecclesial leadership, yet on the other hand Paul, in the greetings of Romans 16, recognizes women as equal partners with men in exercising all the roles of church leadership.

For a long time, the solution of a canon-within-the-canon has emerged as a practical necessity, whether it is articulated theologically ("that which commends Christ") or pragmatically ("that which is life-giving, liberating, and loving," or "I don't like Paul so I don't bother with him"). Others have protested that defaulting to a canon-within-the-canon approach is too selective and preempts the richness of the canon's diversity. The metaphor of a "conversation among diverse voices," it has been suggested, invites believing communities in their particular circumstances into an engagement with the numerous voices or perspectives of the canon. Whichever approach is employed, the canon permits diverse perspectives and practices.

Whether a canon-within-the-canon approach or the invitation-to-a-conversation model is adopted to negotiate the canon's diversity, a third issue emerges for contemporary communities: What about relevance? One of the factors influencing the acceptance of writings into the canon involved churches finding writings relevant to a wide range of circumstances and situations. Some contemporary readers have continued to press the question of relevance. We observed above that the great Protestant reformer Martin Luther wanted to exclude several writings from the canon in the sixteenth century because he did not think they were sufficiently christological in their content.

In our own time, questions about relevance have been posed in several forms. In finishing this chapter, I will report two such questions. I will also identify a variety of ways people have engaged these questions.

Here's the first question:

- Can old documents, writings that are two thousand years old, have much to say to our contemporary world of genetic engineering, high-tech communication, nuclear weapons, reproductive issues, and space travel? These issues didn't exist in the ancient world. Is there any connection? If so, where and how?

Some might respond by saying that to ask such a question is illegitimate. The Bible is God's Word, and we should accept it as more than adequate for any human situation. That is certainly one response. But for some both outside and inside the communities of faith, that confession would raise as many questions as it answers. They would want a less confessional and more thoughtful response.

In response to the question, some might argue that the canon of New Testament writings is not as concerned with issues such as high-tech communication as it is with identity. It is not a rent-a-verse collection, dispensing a pithy one-liner for any human question or issue. Rather, it is about a framework, an orientation to a way of engaging life from a particular identity or perspective;

it is life lived in relation to God. The canon frames, but cannot substitute for, the journey of engagement that human living requires. So even if the New Testament writers know nothing about aspects of how we "do" life in our world, they do identify matters of central importance about human existence and identity at any time in any place.

Others might argue that we need to take a long-term, big-picture view of the canon. The canon is not just about our time and our church: instead, it is about all of time and the church everywhere in every place. It has to function for the church in every age. Some parts of it will particularly address some times and circumstances but not other times and circumstances.

Another question has been asked in some parts of the contemporary church:

- Can documents selected through a very human process be adequate for the task assigned to them as the church's Scriptures?

Some have observed that fine documents widely used in the early churches were rejected by the leaders who ratified the canon. As we have seen, many favorites did not make it, such as the *Didache* or the *Acts of Paul and Thecla*. It is undeniable that the cultural location, gender, investment in power, and social conditioning of these ratifying leaders influenced their choices. They often chose hierarchy-legitimating documents. They opted for institutions rather than spiritual gifts, favored men over women, and preferred stable doctrinal formulation rather than openness and experience. Some of these might be false alternatives, but there is no doubt that the five-stage process outlined above was a very human one.

Some have said that no matter how human the process was, nevertheless God's Spirit was watching over it and guarding it. Some have said that having a *collection* of writings means that other writings in the canon provide a corrective perspective (canon-within-the-canon). Some have wondered whether the canon-selecting process should be reopened, allowing for reconsideration of numerous ancient documents that did not make it the first time around. Others have suggested that writings from across the ages since 397 CE and from contemporary times and societies should be considered as possible sources of new revelation. They argue that while the canon provides an important link to the past, it does so at the expense of connection with the present and human life lived in relation to God now. Others have said that any such attempts would be impossible to organize and illegitimate to carry out. The closed canon, they argue, provides a continuity for the church for all time. Every generation again affirms the canon and takes its place in, and gains its identity from, this great line of witnesses.

Conclusion

The canon of New Testament writings has continued to function for churches across two thousand years, but it has not done so without question and debate. It has put in place boundaries while also legitimating diversity and multiplicity of practices and understandings within the Jesus tradition and communities. It has taken writings that were shaped by the various and specific worlds out of which the New Testament was formed and delivered them to very different worlds and contemporary contexts.

CONCLUSION

$\mathcal{B}$ack on the first page of the introduction, I raised the question about the payoff to reading this book. I gave a short answer to that question:

The seven chapters of this book provide an orientation to some important aspects of the early Jesus movement and the New Testament. Reading it will enlighten you about the beginnings of the Christian movement and help your understanding of the New Testament.

Throughout, I have suggested that seven events embracing

- Hellenistic culture (the death of Alexander, 323 BCE),
- the process of the translation of the Septuagint (ca. 250s BCE*),
- Jewish vibrancy and diversity (the rededication of the temple, 164 BCE),
- Roman imperial power (Pompey's control of Judea, 63 BCE),
- the crucifixion of Jesus (ca. 30 CE),
- the writing of numerous documents by Jesus-believers (the New Testament writings, ca. 50–ca. 130 CE),
- and the process of the formation of the canon (its "closing," 397 CE)

compose the worlds from which the New Testament emerged. These worlds shaped its origins and continue to impact contemporary interpretation of it.

In this final chapter I want to highlight briefly seven dynamics that I think are important for understanding the New Testament and the worlds from which it emerged. These dynamics have surfaced for me from our previous discussions. Here I am looking back over the seven events we have discussed in this book with an eye on the implications of these observations for our contemporary

155

context and engagement with the New Testament. These observations do not assume that someone is or is not a religious believer, though the last one has a particular edge to it for those who claim to be contemporary Jesus-believers. Nor do I assume that every reader of this book would or should identify these particular dynamics. I offer them for your reflection and consideration. Because the New Testament writings are very important for believing communities, how they are read in those communities matters very much.

So here are my seven important dynamics for understanding the New Testament:

First, the New Testament writings did not drop out of the sky one day untouched by human culture, minds, experiences, history, politics, and communities. Their content and its expression are very connected to, embedded in, and reflective of the cultural and historical realities of their time. We have identified some of the complexities and structures of those times from which they emerged. We have discussed the multilayered worlds of Hellenistic culture, Jewish traditions and practices, and Roman power. We have seen that, far from being disconnected from these worlds, the New Testament writings are influenced by them, embrace them, resist them, and address them. Interpreting the New Testament writings—including trying to live a life shaped by them—without taking into account cultural and historical realities not only misses integral dimensions of the texts, but also ignores important aspects of the lives that they seek to shape.

Second, the New Testament writings emerge from a multicultural world. This recognition is closely connected to the previous observation. The New Testament writings do not adopt a bunker mentality and try to escape their complex and multicultural world. They provide diverse examples of Jesus-believers wrestling with how to understand themselves and their commitments to God's purposes in the context of such a world. The affirmation that the God of Jesus is the gracious God of all peoples is one that emerges through various conflicts and disputes and is informed by particular Jewish cultural traditions. Reading the New Testament also means recognizing that in places the writings do not faithfully embrace their own inclusive vision. They are not always gracious to women, to people of various sexual orientations, to slaves, to Jewish folks, and to outsiders or those who are not Jesus-believers. Since they emerge from human beings in particular cultural contexts, such treatment is understandable, but it does not require that contemporary readers continue it. Contemporary readers need to discern when to read against the grain.

Third, the New Testament writings draw on and recycle Jewish traditions and practices. Both of those verbs—draw on and recycle—are very important. As we have seen, New Testament writers borrow lots of images and paradigms from the Jewish Scriptures—in Greek, of course (the Septuagint)—but they do so by reading with their Jesus-glasses on. The New Testament writings show that Jesus-believers exist very much in continuity with God's continuing relationship with Israel, yet also in discontinuity because of claims about Jesus. Their Jesus-centered interpretations existed alongside other readings or interpretations of the same Scriptures that had nothing to do with Jesus. Clearly the commitments and circumstances of interpreters of sacred writings impact the meanings that they make from these writings. Regrettably, some New Testament writings lose sight of this continuity with Jewish traditions, become forgetful of God's covenant commitment to Israel, and seem to claim an exclusive place for Jesus-believers only. New Testament writings are indebted to Jewish cultural and theological traditions.

Fourth, the New Testament writings engage and reflect the Roman imperial world. As followers of Jesus crucified by Rome and its allies (the ruling group in Jerusalem), the writers have to make sense of both Jesus's death and the imperial power that put him to death because he threatened their world. We have seen throughout that in the worlds from which the New Testament writings emerge, religion is tightly enmeshed with politics. They are not separated spheres. The New Testament is very concerned with political matters, with how human societies are organized, with how power is used and for whose benefit, and with how resources are controlled. The New Testament writings thus often have a tensive relationship with Roman power. Sometimes they negotiate it by pragmatically accommodating to it. But sometimes they also dissent from its claims and controls because of their commitment to God as Lord of all and a vision of God's just and life-giving world for all. Ironically, eschatological scenarios in the New Testament writings that assert God's rule over all often imitate the very imperial claims they seek to resist. Contemporary readings of New Testament writings that spiritualize or individualize these writings miss their much wider concern with social structures, societal visions and commitments, and political agenda.

Fifth, the New Testament writings that emerge from these intersecting worlds speak with various voices. They are multiple, diverse, varied, and complex in their perspectives and insights. These diversities reflect the experiences and insights of the various authors and communities from which they emerge. They reflect the multicultural and complex worlds in which the authors lived. They reflect the particular circumstances of the community of Jesus-believers being addressed. The writings do their theological and pastoral work by means of different genres and in different styles, sometimes more narrative, sometimes more propositional. Of course there are some similarities and commonalities among the writings. Commitment to Jesus, the experience of God's presence, the reading of the Jewish Scriptures, life together in communities of believers—these are examples of common emphases. But within each of these categories, there are lots of differences and varieties. As we have seen, groups of believers have different structures and leadership, there are different and numerous interpretations of Jesus's death, there are different understandings of what God is doing in the present and will do in the future. Faithfulness remains a contested value; it can take various forms. Reading the New Testament means not smoothing out and blurring over these diverse perspectives in order to force all the texts to say one thing. Rather, it involves engaging each of the writings on its own terms with its rich variety and diversity.

Sixth, the New Testament writings that emerge from these intersecting worlds are social texts. They emerge from communities of believers; they are directed to and shape communities of believers. The canonization of these writings reflects the same dynamic. The writings that compose the New Testament emerged from communities that used them and found them helpful. The formation of the canon has ensured that they have continued to function for communities across the ages, shaping and guiding their communal life in matters of faith, love, and justice. Both then and now, living in community brings considerable complexity, conflict, and at times contradiction. The writings can lift up marvelous life-giving and just visions of social interactions without the writers always following through on them. Paul, for example, can declare that in Christ there is neither slave nor free, but he does not seem to follow through on that observation by opposing slavery as an institution. For our contemporaries who read the New Testament in a world in which individualism is a central commitment, the recognition of this social dynamic can help our understanding of these ancient but modern writings. It helps us to notice their assumption of communal life, their concern with the quality of relationships and social interactions, and their commitment to embracing all people in communities of love, faith, and hope.

The previous six observations focus on the New Testament writings, but my seventh observation moves the focus from the writings to their readers. At various points in the previous chapters, we have seen how important readers or audiences are. Reading with Jesus-glasses produced readings of the Septuagint that no one else had ever developed. These insights from the biblical paradigms were crucial for early Jesus-believers. Hearing New Testament writings shaped the practices and thinking of communities of Jesus-believers. The same process of hearing and reading was crucial in the centuries that it took for the canon to emerge in the late fourth century.

Through all of this, the historical and cultural circumstances of readers influenced the meanings and interpretations they fashioned from reading these texts. This is how it has always been and always will be. Readers of every generation bring their concerns and circumstances to the New Testament texts to think about their lives in relation to them. This is not a static enterprise but a very active quest to make meaning from the intersection of our lives with these texts. That interaction gives readers a lot of power and requires that readers think carefully about how they read the New Testament. Readers have made these texts say all sorts of things across the ages, some helpful, some destructive. Readers have claimed the authority of the New Testament texts to justify the subjugation of women; the continuation of racist practices like slavery, segregation, and apartheid; militant patriotic fervor; hateful and excluding political agendas; and economic practices that favor a few at the expense of the many. As everyone knows, people can make the Bible say whatever they want it to say. Yet readers have also found in the New Testament writings inspiration to live courageous and loving lives in the service of God, in doing justice and mercy, and in making a huge contribution to improving the world.

Are there any safeguards or guidelines? Reading with awareness of the worlds from which these texts emerged and reading in community help readers to have genuine conversation with the texts and with other readers, rather than simply making the texts reflect our prejudices and preferences. Reading in community requires awareness of how readers are interpreting the texts, what values and practices they are promoting, and who is being harmed and benefited by the interpretation. Reading in community requires conversation and accountability.

INDEX